MARK HARTMANN

SWEAT EQUITY PAYDAY

Sell Your Business Smart.
Hit Your Number.
Exit on Your Terms.

Dedicated to my loving wife, business partner, and favorite travel buddy, **Shelby C. Rhodes** - thank you for your unwavering support, patience, and belief through every long day that went into this book.

Dedicated to **John T. Criscione**, my friend and former business partner at EthiCare Advisors—thank you for making me a better manager, leader, and human being, one day at a time.

Dedicated to **David A. Colavito**, aka "Debits & Credits," my friend, long-time CPA, and a trusted advisor in business and life – thank you for telling me what I need to hear and guiding me to better choices.

Dedicated to **Jason J. Waldstein,** my attorney and true friend - thank you for your creative approach, business-minded counsel, and relentless follow-through that makes you the advisor every business owner hopes to have on speed dial.

Dedicated to all the **lower middle market business owners**—for the daily grind, for being the economic engine of America, and for the purpose behind writing this book. May you be sell-ready, reduce buyer risk, and command a premium so you can walk out vertical on your own terms.

CONTENTS

FOREWORD

by John Warrillow

Author of *Built to Sell, The Automatic Customer,*
and *The Art of Selling Your Business*

I first met Mark Hartmann in 2018 when he joined The Value Builder System™ community. From the beginning, he stood out—not because he was loud or flashy, but because he had been in the trenches. Mark didn't come from academia or theory. He came from the hard reality of building and selling a business with his own sweat and capital on the line.

Before becoming an M&A advisor, Mark built EthiCare Advisors, a cost-containment firm in the insurance industry. He bootstrapped it from scratch, grew it to eight figures, and sold it without outside investment. In other words, Mark lived the exit process before ever advising someone else through it. That experience gave him a unique vantage point—the ability to see the sale not just through the lens of an advisor, but through the heart of a founder.

Since joining the Value Builder community, Mark has helped countless owners prepare for the most important financial event of their lives: the sale of their company. But what separates Mark isn't just technical expertise—it's empathy. He knows that selling a business isn't just a transaction; it's a transfer of identity, legacy, and purpose.

He understands the quiet fear that sits underneath the spreadsheets: What happens to my people? My reputation? My life after this?

That empathy runs through this book. Mark writes with authority but also with humility. He doesn't sugarcoat the process or pretend that every sale is a victory lap. He calls out the pitfalls owners face—the ego, the denial, the messy books, the misplaced trust in a cousin who's never closed a deal. And he does it not to lecture but to prepare you.

His advice is grounded in what I'd call pragmatic realism. For example, Mark's "Kidnap Test" forces you to confront how dependent your business is on you. It's a simple question with a profound implication: if your company can't run without you, it's not a business—it's a job. That test is at the core of what we believe at Built to Sell. Businesses that can thrive without their owners are not only more valuable, they give their founders freedom—before and after an exit.

What I admire most about Mark's writing is how he weaves the emotional, the operational, and the strategic into one narrative. He understands that value isn't created in spreadsheets—it's built in habits. Systems, not heroics. Processes, not personality. That's how you create a business that attracts buyers and commands premium offers.

Over the years, I've seen hundreds of advisors come through our community. A few emerge as true thought leaders—people who not only understand how to calculate value but how to build it. Mark is one of them. His work embodies the mission of The Value Builder System™: to help business owners design companies that are both more valuable and more enjoyable to run.

This book is a reflection of that mission. It's equal parts reality check and roadmap. Mark will challenge you, but he'll also show you a way forward. You'll come away not just with a list of to-dos, but with a deeper understanding of what it really takes to sell your business on your terms.

If you're an owner who has spent years building something from nothing, you'll see yourself in these pages. And if you've ever wondered what it would take to walk away proud—financially, emotionally, and personally ready—Mark's experience will light the path.

— John Warrillow
Founder, The Value Builder System™
Toronto, Canada

INTRODUCTION

If you're like most business owners approaching retirement, you've probably had this quiet thought: *"If I could snap my fingers and make this business sale go exactly the way I want, what would that look like?"*

Let me tell you what I hear over and over again from people in your shoes who've spent 20, 30, and sometimes even 40 years building something meaningful. They want to walk away confidently, knowing that they "hit their number," the one they need to fund the lifestyle they've worked so hard to enjoy in retirement.

They want to ensure their legacy—their people, their name, their reputation—will be respected and preserved. The new owner won't run the business into the ground. Employees will still have jobs, customers will continue to be cared for, and the brand will uphold the same values on which it was built.

Believe it or not, it's possible, but only if you prepare for it.

The majority of owners only sell a business once in their lives. They build one company, pour everything into it, and when it's time to sell, it's uncharted territory. This isn't something they've done before, and odds are, they're not planning to do it again. So naturally, they're scared of not getting what the business is actually worth and leaving money on the table.

And there's the cost. Selling a business isn't cheap. You've got to pay your lawyer, your accountant, your M&A advisor—it adds up.

And if it doesn't go well, it feels like a gamble. Much of the hesitation stems from uncertainty about who to trust. I joke sometimes—your cousin might be a great divorce attorney, but that doesn't mean he should be handling your business sale. I've seen it too many times: Uncle Larry chimes in with, "Hey, make sure you use Cousin Brucey. He knows contracts." That might work for a prenup, but it's not going to cut it for a business sale. The same goes for your accountant. If they've never handled an M&A transaction, it's going to be a problem, especially when you enter the due diligence phase, where things can unravel fast if the wrong people are in the room.

Another significant fear, especially among men, is around identity. When someone asks you, "Tell me about yourself," the first thing out of your mouth is probably, "I own XYZ Company" or "I run this business." Your business is what you do *and* who you are. So, of course, the idea of handing it over to someone else is scary. What if they don't take care of it? What if they destroy the brand you built? That kind of fear doesn't go away with a big check.

Then there's the doubt that the deal will even go through. If word leaks to your employees, vendors, or customers that you're considering selling, then the deal *doesn't* happen? That can wreck your business in a hurry. If there are employees you *must* let in on the fact that a sale is happening, they better be the right people.

A key employee might jump ship or, worse, try to leverage the situation to their advantage. A vendor could threaten to pull their contract. A major customer might start shopping for backup options, afraid of what a new owner might bring. All of this could leave you limping along in a "handicapped" business if the sale falls apart. And at that point, you're back in the trenches, dealing with broken relationships and rebuilding lost trust.

I hear this one all the time: "My people are like family."

No, they're not. Unless they're literally family by blood or marriage, they're employees. They're there for a paycheck. Now, don't get me wrong, they might love you. They might be loyal. They might show up early and stay late and come to your barbecue every summer. However, when push comes to shove, they will do what is in their best interest. Deep down, most business owners know this, but they are reluctant to admit it out loud.

And, of course, let's not forget the biggest fear of all: *What if I don't get enough for the business?*

I typically encounter two types of owners: one who is *sure* of what the business is worth, based on a chat with their accountant or something they read online. And another who says, "I have no idea. You'll have to tell me."

Here's what happens every time: I run the numbers, do my analysis, and when I come back with the valuation, they're disappointed. It's rarely what they hoped. They thought it was worth more. Always more, not less. I've seen owners who needed double what their business could actually bring in just to maintain the lifestyle they hoped for. Maybe they didn't save enough. Perhaps they didn't plan well. Or maybe they were counting on the business being their big payoff. Either way, that fear of falling short is the one that keeps people stuck.

All of these fears are valid. But they don't have to paralyze you. You just need a better plan and the right guide to walk you through it. If you don't have a deal team—a true M&A advisor, an accountant who knows transactions, and a transaction attorney who's actually closed deals before—it's going to be even harder.

These specialists are skilled at identifying serious buyers. There's a phrase I often use: Buyers are liars. That might sound harsh, but it's reality. The buyer pool today is flooded with people chasing what's called entrepreneurship through acquisition. Some are legit. Many are not. Some are trying to string together a bunch of businesses into a so-called "roll-up" to flip for a higher multiple. Their motivations may or may not be aligned with yours. So, you need people on your side who can distinguish what is real from what is smoke.

Selling to a larger strategic buyer can be intimidating. And the noise out there doesn't help. Between the flood of emails from financial advisors, marketing "gurus," and PR firms, it's no wonder owners feel overwhelmed. Everyone's trying to sell them something, and it gets harder and harder to figure out who's legit and who's just noise.

Additionally, if you're drowning in the day-to-day, you won't have the bandwidth to run a sale process. And that's a problem. If you're too critical to daily operations, that could actually lower the value of your business. Your M&A advisor should act as the quarterback, managing the project, coordinating the players, and keeping things moving. You need to stay focused on running the business at full speed so that when buyers take a look, they see a company that's strong, steady, and ready.

When I sit down with a business owner who's thinking about retirement, they are experiencing all of the above fears and uncertainties, and the same handful of questions almost always come up:

- *"What's my business really worth?"*
- *"How long will it take to sell my business?"*
- *"What should I be doing right now?"*
- *"How do I keep my employees, vendors, and customers from finding out I'm selling?"*
- *"How much will it cost me to hire professionals?"*

If you've asked yourself any or all of these questions, you're not alone. That's exactly why I wrote this book. To help business owners like you get real answers from someone who's been there. I built, bootstrapped, scaled, and sold my own specialized insurance cost containment consulting firm for eight figures. We didn't have investors. We didn't take outside capital. Every dollar that grew the business came from the profits we created. That kind of growth earned us a spot on the *Inc. 5000* list of fastest-growing privately held companies in America for three consecutive years. Twice, we landed in the top 50 in insurance. So, when I discuss building value in a business, I'm not speaking theoretically—I've done it.

Academically, I've got an MBA. I've studied and passed the Certified Mergers & Acquisitions Professional (CM&AP) program. I was one of the early adopters of the Certified Exit Planning Advisor (CEPA) designation, earning that back in 2012. I'm also a Certified Business Intermediary (CBI) and hold other designations that keep me sharp and relevant in this space.

However, more than the credentials, I bring a real-world understanding of what it's like to be a business owner weighing the decision to sell. There's a reason you've put in all those years. The late nights. The tough calls. The sacrifices no one saw. And now you're standing at the edge of something big.

I like to call this moment your *sweat equity payday.*

You've made a good living over the years, but the real reward comes at the sale. That's when you unlock the value you've been building all this time. That deferred payday, the one you've been sitting on for decades, finally arrives. It's the next chapter of your life. That might be travel. That might be golf. That might be time with your kids and grandkids. Whatever it is, that freedom—that choice—is what you've been working for.

And if you do it right, you're walking away with peace of mind, leaving behind a company that can thrive without you, a brand that lives on, and a team that's well taken care of. You're handing over the keys to someone competent, maybe even someone who can grow it further than you ever imagined.

My wish for you is always to be **sell-ready,** even if you're not planning to sell tomorrow. The more educated you are, the smoother this process goes. When someone calls me up and says, "Mark, I want to sell my business," and I ask a few questions, and I realize they're sell-ready, I know they're going to get the results they deserve.

The best exits don't happen by accident. They happen because you prepared for them. So, if you're ready to learn how to position your business for the best possible outcome, confidently hit your number, secure your legacy, and start living the next chapter, you're in the right place.

Let's get started.

- Mark Hartmann

PART ONE

THE DECISION TO SELL

THE
DECISION
TO SELL

CHAPTER ONE
THE INNER TUG-OF-WAR

T he connection between you and your business is unlike anything else in your life. You've poured years, maybe decades, into it. Perhaps you built it from scratch. Maybe you inherited it. Maybe you're the third or fourth generation to carry the torch.

Deciding to sell is probably the toughest decision of your entire life. Timing it right? Nearly impossible. I'm sure you've already heard horror stories from friends—maybe standing around after a round of golf—about deals blowing up halfway through, or someone selling and then watching helplessly as the new owners gutted the company, laid off employees, and trashed the brand they worked so hard to build.

And that fear is real.

There's this voice in the back of your head saying, *"No one is going to run it as well as I do. I'm known for this. I'm the widget guy in this community. What happens to my legacy if someone else ruins it?"*

That's the psychological tug-of-war every owner goes through. And it's something a lot of advisors overlook when they talk about selling a business—they skip right over the emotional weight of it all.

For many of my clients, the conversation eventually comes down to this: *"I've got to retire. I don't want to wait until I'm too old to enjoy what time I have left."*

Selling allows you to unlock the life you've been working toward all these years—more time for golf, travel, family, or whatever your version of *la dolce vita* (the good life) is. But to get there, you need to do it right. You only sell your business once. Make it count. I'll be straight with you—it's the most complex process you will ever go through as a business owner. You need the right team of people around you to get to the closing table, including advisors, attorneys, and accountants. Ideally, these individuals will all understand what is at stake, not only financially, but also emotionally.

The Emotional Roadblocks No One Talks About

If I had to sum up the biggest roadblock for most owners in one word, it's this: **Fear.** It shows up in a lot of ways, but it's always there. Let me walk you through the most common ones, because if you're feeling any of these, you're not alone.

"Is My Business Even Sellable?"

You may question whether your business is even sellable. *Do I really have something worth buying? What's it worth?*

Every business owner has a number in their head—a magic number they think their business is worth. And that number is tied to what that money will mean for you and your family in the next chapter of your life. But until you know the real value of your business, that question—*"Will it get me what I need?"*—lingers in the back of your mind.

"Will I Get What I Think My Business Is Worth?"

This is the big one—money, and it comes in two parts.

The first part is not getting what you think your business is worth. I can't tell you how many times I've asked an owner, *"What's your business worth?"* and they answer, *"Well, I'd like to get five million. Maybe seven. Ten would be great."*

Just because you'd *like* to get it doesn't mean it's worth that.

One of the first things I discuss with owners is obtaining a valuation. Not when you're already packing up to sell, but five to seven years out. You need to know the real number—whether it's one million, four million, or somewhere in between—because that's the only way to build a solid financial plan for your future. Too many owners stick their heads in the sand because they don't want to face that reality. But avoiding it doesn't change the number. Knowing it gives you power.

"Will I Have Enough to Live the Life I Want?"

The second part of the money fear is lifestyle. You've worked hard to build a life you love, and you don't want to sell only to find out you can't afford to live it. Perhaps your dream is to travel the world, cruise across six continents, in first-class luxury all the way. Great. But that world cruise might cost you a quarter million dollars in your first year of retirement. You need to know if your financial plan can handle that and still give you the life you want for the long haul. This is where working with a financial planner—*before* you sell—is critical.

"Do I Have the Right Team?"

I'll be blunt: if you don't have the right team, your deal is over before it even starts. This is one of the first conversations I have with owners. I'll ask, *"Tell me about your accountant. Tell me about your lawyer. What's their transaction experience?"* And a lot of times, I get answers like, *"Oh, I've used the same attorney for years."*

Then I have to explain that you wouldn't go to your general practitioner for brain surgery. Yes, he's a doctor, but you're not going to let him open up your skull. You want a brain surgeon. Selling your business is no different.

You need a transaction attorney who specializes in deals like this. Bonus points if they've worked in your industry, but even if they haven't, a great transaction attorney will have enough experience to handle the nuances. The same goes for your accountant and, yes, your M&A advisor. This is too important to let amateurs learn on the job.

"What Happens to My People?"

And then there's the fear for your employees, especially if you have family members still working in the business. You've built a team, maybe even a work family. What happens to them after you leave?

"What Happens to My Identity?"

The toughest fear to face is what happens to *you* after the sale.

For years, you've been known as "the widget guy" (or whatever your business is). Everybody at Rotary knows you as the widget guy. Everybody at the Chamber calls you when they need widgets. People might not even know your last name. They just know, *"If you need widgets, call Tom."*

So what happens when Tom sells Tom's Widget Company?

Now Larry owns it, but it's still called Tom's Widget Company. Does that tarnish the brand? Will Larry keep your standards, or will he run it into the ground? And if he does, does that reflect on you?

I've experienced this myself. I sold my old company, EthiCare Advisors, over seven years ago, and just the other weekend, someone came up to me and said, *"Hey Mark, how are things at EthiCare Advisors?"* I laughed and told them I hadn't owned it in years, but people don't easily disconnect you from the company. To them, you *are* the company, long after you've moved on.

It reminds me a little of the TV show *Yellowstone*—you know how they brand the ranch hands as a symbol of loyalty? Well, for business owners, that company logo is like a brand burned into your identity. Especially if the company literally carries your name. And that's why letting go is so hard. You're not just selling a business. You're selling a piece of who you are—or at least, who everyone thinks you are.

Letting Go (and Why You May Need to Stick Around)

The good news is that, in most transitions, it's important to stay connected to the business (at least for a little while). I had an owner once who thought he wanted the exact opposite of staying tied to his business. He made it clear: the second the deal closed, he was out. No transition, no sticking around.

The problem was that he was the entire sales department. Every major client relationship went through him. When buyers heard that he planned to leave right after closing, they walked. They weren't just buying a business—they were buying *his* relationships. Without him, the whole thing was worth a fraction of what he thought.

If you want top dollar and the best possible terms, you need to be open to staying involved for a while. In many cases, the best transitions take around a year.

And it makes sense when you think about it. Buyers are paying for the way *you* ran the business. They want you there long enough to teach them how to run it the same way. That doesn't mean you're chained to the place forever, but if you're willing to help the new owner succeed, you'll get a better deal and protect the legacy you've worked so hard to build.

The Myth of Perfect Timing

Now, let me tell you something that a lot of owners don't want to hear:

It is impossible to time the sale of a business.

I can't say this enough. Market conditions change constantly. One day there's a tariff, the next day it's gone, and that wreaks havoc on valuations. Geopolitics, technology, and new competitors can all destroy your business's value almost overnight.

Sure, sometimes people get lucky and hit the "perfect" moment. But that's all it is—luck. There's no skill in timing the market.

If you have a good offer today, and the price and terms work for you, take it seriously. Waiting for "just a little bit more" tomorrow is gambling. And I've seen too many owners lose that bet.

One of the biggest regrets I hear comes from owners who waited because they believed in the myth of perfect timing. They'll tell me, *"Mark, I had this amazing pipeline lined up. It was going to explode four quarters from now. A, B, and C were locked in."*

And then? Something changed. A competitor introduced new technology. A big customer switched vendors. Market shifts, political changes, even global events—any of those can knock the legs out from under a business.

If you've got an offer that works, don't let fear or greed convince you to wait for something that may never come.

Defining Your Next Chapter

When I sit down with a business owner, one of the first things I ask is a simple question: *"What does retirement look like compared to your life right now?"*

I want to know what you really want. Do you picture yourself on a world cruise three months after closing? Buying a beach house where the grandkids come every weekend next summer? Playing 100 rounds of golf next year because you finally have the time? Or maybe it's something as simple as taking every Friday off to spend with family.

The sale needs to be structured in a way that gets you there. That means finding the right buyer who can give you the terms and transition you need to make that next chapter possible. However, to do that, you must be honest with yourself about what you truly want.

"I Just Don't Know If I'm Ready..."

If you feel like you're not ready, ask yourself these questions:

1. *"Why do I think that I'm not ready right now?"*
2. *"What's holding me back?"*
3. *"What do I need to do to feel ready, and how long will it take to get there?"*

More often than not, the *business* is ready. The *owner* isn't. I've sat across from people with great companies—businesses that are well-run, profitable, and absolutely sellable, and they're still stuck in "I don't know, I don't know, I don't know."

When we unpack it, the same fears keep coming up. What will happen to the brand? Will the employees be treated well? Will I get enough money to live the life I want?

And that's okay. Those are valid questions. But ignoring them doesn't make them go away. Talking about them honestly is the first step in moving forward.

If you're feeling torn right now, it's normal. In fact, I'd be worried if you *weren't* wrestling with this decision. But here's what I can tell you from sitting across the table from hundreds of owners: clarity comes when you start asking yourself the hard questions. What do you want your life to look like after this? What would make you feel good, not just about the check you cash, but about the legacy you leave behind?

The tug-of-war doesn't disappear overnight, but it does get quieter when you're honest with yourself. And once you can picture that next chapter clearly, the decision to sell stops feeling like an ending and starts feeling like the beginning of something you've earned.

KEY TAKEAWAYS

- Selling your business is as much an emotional decision as a financial one—fears about money, legacy, and identity are normal, but facing them head-on is the only way to move forward.
- Knowing the actual value of your business early gives you power; guessing or waiting for "perfect timing" is just gambling with your future.
- The right team of experienced transaction professionals can make or break your deal—this isn't the time for amateurs to learn on the job.

- Being open to staying involved after the sale often leads to better terms, a smoother transition, and protects the legacy you've built.
- Clarity comes when you're honest with yourself about what you want your life to look like after the sale; once you can picture that future, letting go feels less like losing and more like finally winning the life you worked for.

CHAPTER TWO

WHAT HAPPENS IF YOU'RE NOT READY

've said this before, and I'll say it again: timing your sale is nearly impossible. If you think you're going to call the top of the market like some kind of exit-strategy day trader, you're incorrect. And if you do happen to get the timing exactly right, it had nothing to do with you. That was just luck. I'm a firm believer in that.

I've lived it, too. Years ago, I owned a company called EthiCare Advisors, and someone came to me with an offer to buy it. At the time, I hadn't given exit planning much thought, because like most owners, I was too busy running the business to even think about selling it. But the unsolicited offer forced me to take it seriously.

The financial buyer offered me three times EBITDA on a three-year earnout. That meant I'd have to stay on for three years, essentially handing over the company and working like an employee. And at the end of that earnout, they'd get the company, and I'd end up with what I probably would have made anyway over those three years.

That experience made me realize I wasn't ready. I was the hub and spoke of the entire company. I was the chief cook and bottle washer. I was doing sales. I was running operations. I was the face of everything. If I had walked out the door, the business would have crumbled.

If that sounds like your business today, pay attention.

I had to get serious about building something that didn't revolve around me. I had to grow the business in a way that made me replaceable and it valuable. I had to take myself out of those roles. That's when things started to change. I started working on the business, and not just in the business.

That decision led to a windfall several years later.

Even after all that, I still think I sold too early. I did very well—I had an eight-figure exit—but if I had sold just one year later, I believe I would've added several million dollars to the deal. But again, you can't time it. You can't sit around waiting for the perfect market conditions. You can't wait for everything to align. Because the truth is, something will always come up, personally or professionally, that forces your hand. And that's the problem with not being ready.

You have to be ready before someone comes knocking. You can't wait until you *need* to sell. Don't let one of the dreaded Ds—Death, Divorce, Disability, Distress, or Disagreement—be the reason you start thinking about an exit.

Being exit-ready means you're in control of the timing even when the timing isn't perfect. And it means that when the right buyer does show up, you can move forward confidently on your terms, not theirs.

Mistakes That Cost You

One of the biggest disconnects I see is this: Sellers want premium prices and terms, but they haven't done the work to actually earn them. Here are some common mistakes to avoid:

Mistake #1: You *Are* the Business

If you're still running everything—operations, sales, you name it—you're not ready to sell, at least not for a premium. At best, you're looking at an earnout, or a deal that keeps you tied to the business for a year or two after the sale because there's no one else to run it. I don't care how good your numbers look—if the buyer sees that *you* are the one generating all the revenue, they're going to structure the deal so you stay on.

You need to build a team that can carry on without you. Two to three years before you think about selling, begin transitioning sales responsibilities. Bring in or elevate someone internally. Let them take over key accounts. Help your clients become comfortable working with someone other than you. That way, when the business sells, it still runs smoothly and the value stays intact. That's what gives buyers confidence and allows you to step away without dragging down the price or the terms.

Mistake #2: Messy Books

I can't tell you how many owners treat their business like a personal piggy bank. They run every non-essential vacation, car, boat, and airplane through it. That kind of accounting muddies the waters when you go to sell.

I always recommend getting your financial house in order two to three years ahead of time. Clean up the books, work with an accounting firm. Better yet, get reviewed financial statements from your CPA. The outside validation gives buyers confidence that what they're seeing is real. It says, *"I'm not hiding anything. These numbers are clean. My accountant agrees."*

Mistake #3: Flying Blind

You need to know your number. I'm not a financial planner, but I know this much: if you don't know what you need to net from your sale to live the lifestyle you want in retirement, you're flying blind. Whether you're dreaming of moving to Florida, spending time with grandkids, or just finally relaxing, a solid personal financial plan will help you define what a successful sale looks like for you. If you don't know that number, how do you know if any offer is good enough?

Mistake #4: Lack of Customer Diversification

If one customer accounts for more than 20–25% of your revenue, that's a red flag. Even worse is when that customer represents a disproportionate amount of your profit. I've seen deals fall apart or valuations get slashed because one "golden goose" customer made up 10% of revenue but 40% of profits. Buyers don't want to take on that risk. And if they do, they're going to make sure it's reflected in the price and terms they offer you.

In some cases, customer concentration isn't fixable—not in the short term. That's why I tell owners: if you've got a few years before you plan to sell, start now. Diversify your client base.

Mistake #5: Overdependence on a Vendor or Supplier

This is another issue that frequently arises, especially with manufacturers.

If there's a proprietary piece or critical component of your product and you're relying on one vendor to supply it, that's a problem. Buyers don't want to be at the mercy of your supplier's whims, delays, or pricing changes. They want options and redundancy.

So if you've only got one vendor for a key piece of your operation, get a second or third lined up well before you go to market. It shows foresight and protects your valuation.

Mistake #6: Bad Timing

Now, I've already said that timing a sale is impossible. But *bad* timing should be avoided at all costs.

Let me give you an example. Say your company's coming off a slow quarter. Maybe you had a hiccup in your sales cycle. Perhaps you were impacted by broader economic shifts—an election year, new tariffs, regulatory changes. We saw it happen in 2025. There was considerable hesitation among business owners during the presidential transition, partly due to concerns about tariffs. And that uncertainty translated into softer numbers.

Imagine you list your business during that dip. By the time April rolls around, the Q1 numbers are in, and they're down. You've just handed a buyer a reason to lower their offer or walk away. That's what bad timing looks like.

Again, you can't control the market. But you *can* be smart about when you list. If you know there's a dip coming or you just came out of one, it might make sense to hold off, fix what needs fixing, and ride the next wave up before selling.

Mistake #7: Thinking Your Business is Immune

Change is constant. Take funeral homes. More people are dying than ever before. But even that industry has changed dramatically. Why? Private equity. In the last few decades, PE firms have rolled up the space, consolidated operators, and transformed the model.

Same thing with HVAC. Ten years ago, it was a different world. Now you've got HVAC companies selling subscription services, offering annual maintenance plans, rolling trucks like clockwork, all pushed by private equity roll-ups and new technology.

Even the so-called "safe" industries aren't safe. Bookstores got eaten alive by Amazon. New industries, like AI and machine learning, weren't even part of the conversation five years ago, and now they're changing everything.

Don't think your business won't be affected. It will. It's just a matter of when and how prepared you are when it happens.

Due Diligence: Where Gaps Get Exposed

One of the most significant mistakes a seller can make, and therefore deserving of its own section in this chapter, is not being ready for due diligence. I always tell my sellers the moment we move forward with a listing:

"In God we trust. Everyone else? Prepare for due diligence."

I don't remember where I first heard it, but I've been saying it ever since. Because it's true. Due diligence is not for the faint of heart. It's emotionally exhausting for both sides, but especially for sellers.

Buyers will ask the same question six different ways, and that drives sellers nuts. They'll say, *"Mark, we already answered this!"* And I'll have to remind them, *"Yeah, but they asked it differently this time. We've got to answer it again, the way they need it."*

This phase of the process is where the cracks show. It's where buyers peel back every layer of the business and start nitpicking everything on purpose. That's their job. They're trying to mitigate risk. And if you're not ready, they'll find the holes.

I once had a deal where a public company was buying a private company—a very well-run business, I might add. I'd give it 90 out of 100—four stars out of five, maybe even four and a half. The operations were strong, the financials were solid, and things looked great on the surface.

But during diligence, the buyer uncovered some gaps in internal HR compliance. Not major lawsuits or criminal behavior, just sloppy documentation, inconsistent policies, and other things a public company simply can't ignore.

That gap caused serious friction. The seller didn't think it was all that concerning. He was like, *"Come on, we've been running this way for years."* But the buyer said, *"Nope. We can't move forward until this is cleaned up."*

It stalled the deal.

And I had to step in, not just as the advisor, but as the referee. I helped both sides stay calm. I acted as a shoulder to cry on when things got tough—and believe me, in diligence, they often do.

In the end, we got the seller to make the necessary changes. The buyer came back to the table and the sale closed. But it was a good reminder that even *well-run companies* can trip during diligence.

Don't take diligence personally. Expect buyers to dig and find something. The more you prepare in advance—years in advance, ideally—the fewer surprises you'll face when it matters most. The goal is to proactively address those gaps, rather than reacting to them under pressure.

Deal Fatigue

Speaking of pressure, deal fatigue sets in when one side—or both—starts to feel like things are dragging on forever. The energy and enthusiasm begin to fade. You've been reviewing documents, answering questions, going back and forth on terms, and somewhere along the line, you feel like, *"Why am I even doing this?"*

If the seller starts getting burned out during diligence, things can get sloppy. You start responding more slowly. You push off meetings. You don't push your advisors to keep things moving. Buyers notice that. And the longer the process drags on, the more likely it is that someone—usually the buyer—gets cold feet. You must be mentally prepared for the process and maintain a positive momentum to complete the deal.

Overconfidence Can Blind You

Burnout isn't the only threat—overconfidence can be just as harmful. If you come in thinking your business is perfect, your numbers are phenomenal, and the buyer should be lucky just to be talking to you, it's easy to overlook the details. You assume nothing will go wrong. You dismiss red flags. You don't take your advisor's advice. That's when deals fall apart—or worse, close at a far lower price than you imagined.

Confidence is good. Arrogance is dangerous. Stay sharp. Stay open. Don't let overconfidence cost you everything you've built.

Why Sell-Ready Is the Only Smart Move

There's a saying I come back to all the time: *"Man makes plans, and God laughs."*

You can have the best intentions. You can think you've got time. But the truth is, there are always external forces in the universe that can flip your plans upside down. And that's why I believe every owner should be sell-ready—even if you don't plan on selling anytime soon.

The Five Ds Are Real and Relentless

Life doesn't care about your five-year plan. The **Five Ds** are the biggest threats to an unplanned exit:

- **Death**
- **Divorce**
- **Disagreement** (with a partner, customer, or top employee)
- **Disability**
- **Distress**

It could be a personal health issue, a fallout with your business partner, or a top employee leaving with key relationships. Or maybe your whole industry takes a hit because of tariffs, economic downturn, or new technology. You can't plan for those things. But you *can* be ready.

In my world, the most common scenarios are what I call "age-related disability" and industry distress. And they often go hand-in-hand. I often see owners who are just worn out. They're not *technically* disabled, but they're not working 50-hour weeks anymore, either. They're slowing down. They've been doing this a long time, and they're tired. Then the industry hits a soft patch. Maybe the economy shifts, or competition ramps up. And now you've got a valuation problem.

They weren't ready. And that slowdown—combined with distress—means they'll get a lower price, guaranteed.

Don't Wait for the 5 Ds

A long time ago—in a galaxy not that far away—a family member of mine had a successful consulting firm with a great team and strong client relationships. But he was the face of the business, especially when it came to sales.

Then disability struck. He was forced to sell quickly. The business could still operate without him, which helped, but the buyers knew he had to sell. They smelled blood in the water.

He got a fair multiple. But if he could've stuck around another year or two? He probably would've gotten **twice** as much. He didn't have everything dialed in. He wasn't truly ready. And because of that, he didn't get to sell on his terms. He didn't get his number. And he had to live with that regret.

Don't wait for death, divorce, disagreement, disability, or distress to force your hand.

The best exits happen when the seller is in control of the timing, the terms, and the process. You deserve that kind of exit. But you have to be ready.

Are You Deal-Ready?

*Ask yourself these five questions to know
if you're truly ready to sell.*

1. Do you know what your business is worth?

❏ Yes   ❏ No

Have you had your business valued by an M&A professional in the last 12 months?

> You can't sell for top dollar if you don't know what you're worth—or why you're worth it. It's important to start with a sellability analysis and valuation to make sure there are no surprises or disappointments later on.

2. Are your finances clean, accurate, and professionally prepared?

❏ Yes   ❏ No

> Accurate, defensible financials are the foundation of an ideal sale. If your books raise questions, so will your valuation. Sloppy financials are one of the fastest ways to scare off a buyer—or give them a reason to slash the price.

3. Could your business survive without you for a week? A month? A quarter?

❏ Yes   ❏ No

> Buyers want businesses, not jobs. If you're still the glue holding everything together, then you're not deal-ready. You'll either have to stay on longer than you want or take a lower offer. The less dependent your company is on you, the more valuable it becomes.

4. Do you have a clear picture of what you want after the sale—both personally and financially?

❏ Yes   ❏ No

> A successful exit requires clarity about what comes next. Without it, it's impossible to define what a "good deal" really looks like for you.

5. Are you emotionally ready to let go?

❏ Yes   ❏ No

> This might be the hardest question of them all. Are you really ready to give up control? Are you prepared to hand off your legacy? Be honest. Because if you're not there mentally, it's going to show—and it's going to get in the way of the best possible outcome.

KEY TAKEAWAYS

- You can't time the market, so you must be ready to sell before life or circumstance forces your hand.
- If your business is centered around you, has disorganized financial records, or relies heavily on a single customer or vendor, buyers will likely lower their offer or tie you to the business post-sale.
- Failing to prepare for due diligence—where every crack gets exposed—is one of the fastest ways to stall or kill a deal.
- Overconfidence and deal fatigue are silent killers in the sales process; stay humble, stay sharp, and stay energized through the finish line.

PART TWO

BUILDING A BUSINESS THAT SELLS

CHAPTER THREE

WHAT'S YOUR BUSINESS ACTUALLY WORTH?

recently got off a 40-minute call with a seller who was in tears. And I'm not joking when I say this—two-thirds of what I do feels like psychotherapy some days. And if you're reading this book because you're starting to think about selling, then you absolutely need to hear this part.

Let's begin with a quote from someone who knows a thing or two about value—Warren Buffett, the Oracle of Omaha. He once said, *"Price is what you pay. Value is what you get."*

That might be one of the most iconic quotes on this entire subject. But for some reason, it's not something enough business owners think about when they're on the selling side of the deal.

Buyers? Sure. They're constantly thinking in terms of value. *What am I really getting for my money?* But as a seller, you need to flip that lens and ask: *What am I actually offering? What is my business really worth to someone else—not just in my eyes, but in the market's eyes?"* Understanding your value—and how others see it—is everything when it comes to getting the outcome you deserve.

Nine times out of ten—maybe even ten out of ten—business owners overvalue their companies. You've poured years, maybe decades, into building your business. You've made sacrifices. You've weathered storms. You've built relationships, created jobs, and kept the lights on when no one else could've. That emotional attachment creates what one of my favorite mentors calls *head trash.*

There's a lot of that out there. And it's usually fed by country club locker room talk. You finish a round of golf and hear that one of your buddies just sold his business for some jaw-dropping number—seven, maybe eight figures. And you start thinking, *Well, shoot—if that guy got that much, my business has to be worth at least that.* This is the kind of noise that gets in the way of clear thinking.

The Truth About Multiples (And Why They're Not What You Think)

One of the most common myths is the idea that there's one fixed "multiple" for every business. Multiples change. They change based on revenue. They change based on earnings. They change based on industry. They even change based on geography.

For example, a business doing $1 million in EBITDA is going to fetch a significantly higher multiple than one doing $300,000, even if the smaller business has a higher margin, because size matters. Private equity groups and strategic buyers are often looking for businesses with *at least* $1 million in EBITDA before they even step into the ring.

So if you've got a $5 million business with $1 million in earnings, your multiple might be way more favorable than a $1 million business with $300,000 in earnings, even if the percentage margin looks better on paper.

Beyond top-line or bottom-line numbers, you must consider *who's buying* and *why they're buying.* A roll-up strategy from a private equity firm is a whole different animal than an individual buyer looking to step into your shoes.

Price and Terms

Here's another place where sellers get tripped up: thinking price is the only number that matters. Let's say someone offers you $10 million for your business. That sounds great, right? But what are the terms?

- Are they buying assets or stock?
- Is the full $10 million paid at closing?
- Or is it $5 million now and $5 million over five years… if certain things go right?

Different deal structures have dramatically different tax consequences. That same $10 million could mean very different things depending on whether it's taxed as capital gains or ordinary income or whether it even shows up in your account at all.

A $10 million price tag with terrible terms isn't worth celebrating. And a $7 million offer with the proper structure might actually net you more in the end. That's why I always say: it's about price *and* terms.

"Buyers Are Liars—and Sellers Are Worse"

There's an old saying that gets thrown around a lot in sales and real estate: *"Buyers are liars."*

But the full version? *"Buyers are liars, and sellers are worse."*

This saying comes from years of dealing with people who say one thing and then do another. A buyer might tell you they're serious and ready to move fast, only to vanish or change course when the numbers hit the table. Sellers can be just as bad—hiding problems, exaggerating earnings, or promising to "stick around" post-sale with zero intention of doing so.

It's not dishonesty in the malicious sense. It's more *selective truth-telling*. People frame things in the best possible light, especially when big money is on the line. But that's exactly why it's so important to dig deeper.

A big part of my job as an M&A advisor is to get past the surface-level B.S. I don't just work with sellers—I spend a lot of time with the buyers, too. If you're interested in my listing, Mr. Buyer, let's talk. *Why* does this business interest you? What *specifically* appeals to you? And just as important—what don't you like? What's holding you back?

I drill down on those questions because the answers help shape the deal. They surface hidden concerns. They also uncover negotiating leverage. And that's the value a good M&A advisor brings to the table—not just matchmaking, but mediation, clarity, and truth.

Because in this world, if you take everything at face value, you'll lose.

The Two Buyer Types

In my opinion, these buyers whom we have to question fall into one of two categories:

Financial Buyers

Financial buyers are in it for one reason: return on investment. They're looking at your business like an asset that generates cash flow today that they can eventually sell for more down the road.

Here's how they think:

- **They care about historical EBITDA and seller's discretionary earnings (SDE).**
- **They care about future cash flow projections.**
- **They care about how quickly they can earn back their investment and make a profit on the exit.**

Most of the time, a financial buyer will keep the current management team in place. They'll run the business "as is" for 6 to 12 months, just observing how things work before making any major changes. They're cautious, calculated, and ROI-driven.

So if your financials are a mess or your profitability is weak, you're going to have a tough time convincing a financial buyer to pay a premium.

Strategic Buyers

Strategic buyers are looking for **synergy**—that magic overlap where your business makes theirs stronger. That could mean:

- **Cost savings** (cutting redundant expenses),
- **Market expansion** (reaching new regions or customers),
- **Competitive advantage** (locking up a key supplier, product, or customer base).

Because of that synergy, a strategic buyer might actually pay **more** than a financial buyer. Their valuation can include a premium based on how well your business fits into their bigger picture.

But here's the tradeoff—they'll move fast. Their integration plan is usually much more aggressive. They want to merge teams, systems, and customer bases quickly. If you're emotionally attached to the way your business runs today, or your people are like family to you, that kind of deal might feel like a gut punch.

Know Who You're Dealing With

The same business can be seen in two completely different lights depending on who's looking at it. A financial buyer might see it as a stable, cash-flowing asset. A strategic buyer might see it as the missing puzzle piece that helps them dominate a market.

The three pillars of sale-ready value are one of my favorite things to walk sellers through because it cuts to the heart of what buyers are looking for.

If you want top dollar for your business—or even just a smooth exit—you need to focus on three things: **profitability, predictability,** and **transferability.**

1. Profitability: More Than Just a Good Year

Yes, buyers want to see strong financials—but it's not just about top-line revenue or a strong P&L for the last 12 months.

It's about:

- **Healthy margins.**
- **Efficient operations.**
- **Scalable growth potential.**

Buyers want to know they're going to get a real return on investment, not inherit a high-maintenance job with unpredictable income. Strong profitability sends the signal that this business isn't in survival mode.

2. Predictability: Can You Count on It?

Next up is predictability. Buyers want to know what they're getting, not take a gamble.

That means:

- **Reliable, consistent revenue.**
- **Systems and processes that produce repeatable results.**
- **Forecasts they can trust.**

If your business has wild revenue swings, seasonal surprises, or key data you can't explain, that's a problem. Predictability builds confidence, which translates into higher offers.

3. Transferability: Can It Run Without You?

As discussed in Chapter Two, this is all about whether the business can keep operating—and growing—without you.

Buyers are asking:

- **Are there systems in place?**
- **Is there a team that knows how to execute?**
- **Are key customer and vendor relationships integrated into the business, rather than just tied to the owner?**

If the whole thing falls apart the minute you walk away, then you are merely selling a *job*.

From Three Years to 60 Days

I've talked before about my prior company, EthiCare Advisors. We received an unsolicited offer that was three times earnings, and it came with a three-year earnout. That meant I'd have to stick around full-time for three more years just to unlock the full sale price.

What changed everything was when I started to take *exit planning* seriously. My team didn't even realize that's what we were doing, but that's exactly what was happening behind the scenes. We started putting systems in place. We built out a team. We documented the processes. We made the business *less about me* and more about the company itself.

Eventually, I sold EthiCare to a strategic buyer backed by private equity. And my transition agreement was just 60 days of full-time work. After that, I was more or less out. No three-year handcuffs. No drawn-out earnout. That's what happens when you build your business around profitability, predictability, and transferability. You get more money *and* more freedom.

Practical Ways to Increase Your Value–Starting Now

So how do you get there? Here's what I recommend as a starting point for each of the three pillars:

PROFITABILITY

- **Clean up your books.**
  Get them reviewed by a CPA—not just internally prepared, but *reviewed*. When I can say to a buyer, "These are CPA-reviewed financials," it builds instant credibility.

- **Stop using the business as a piggy bank.**
  Excessive discretionary spending muddies the water and lowers the perceived value of your business.

PREDICTABILITY

- **Diversify your customer base.**
  If your top five or ten accounts represent a large percentage of revenue, that's a risk. Start spreading it out.

- **Lock in contracts.**
  If your industry allows for it, get customer contracts signed—and push for multi-year agreements. Buyers love seeing that kind of revenue visibility.

TRANSFERABILITY

- **Build a leadership team.**
  Get a solid sales and management team in place that can run the business without you. The faster a buyer believes they can remove you from the equation, the higher the multiple you're going to command.

Value, in the eyes of a buyer, is built on facts: clean financials, repeatable systems, transferable leadership, and a clear runway for growth. If you want to hit your number and enjoy the life that comes after, you've got to do more than *hope* your business is worth what you think it is. You've got to *prove* it.

And the best time to start proving it is right now.

KEY TAKEAWAYS

- Most business owners overestimate their company's value due to emotional attachment and misleading comparisons. The true market value is based on what a buyer sees, not what you feel.
- Valuation multiples vary by size, industry, and buyer type, and a higher top-line doesn't always mean a better deal—context matters.

- It's important to think beyond the purchase price. The terms, tax treatment, and structure of the deal can all drastically change your outcome.
- Financial and strategic buyers value different things; knowing who you're negotiating with helps you position your business for maximum appeal.
- To command top dollar and exit cleanly, focus on profitability, predictability, and transferability—and start building around those pillars now.

CHAPTER FOUR

NEGOTIATE LIKE A TERRORIST

'␣ve said this tongue-in-cheek for a long time—probably 15 or 20 years now. "Negotiate like a terrorist." I don't mean it literally, of course, but there's truth in the lesson. The biggest thing I learned in the trenches of negotiating is this: *"No" is often just the starting point, not the end of the conversation.*

Back when I owned EthiCare Advisors, we worked with health insurance companies to review medical claims. Our job was to identify overcharges, billing and coding errors, duplicates—things that shouldn't have been on the bill in the first place. We also benchmarked costs using our actual claim databases to determine if a hospital or other healthcare provider was charging a fair price for that procedure in that geographic region.

Once we had the evidence, we'd call the provider and say, *"We've identified some billing and coding issues. Let's negotiate a settlement."* That's when I realized something important: finding the person with the authority to say no was just the beginning of the negotiation.

Customer service reps and front-line staff were programmed to say no. That was their job. But I learned to peel back the onion: *"Who has the authority to say yes?"* That's when the real negotiation began.

So, when I say *"negotiate like a terrorist,"* the point is that you shouldn't take no for an answer. Get to the right person, the one who actually has the power to decide.

The Long Game of Selling a Business

Now, let's talk about selling your business because this is where the metaphor really fits. Selling a business is the hardest deal you'll ever go through. It will test you emotionally. Honestly, it might even test you physically, because the process is a grind: 60, 90, even 120 days of back-and-forth with the buyer before you finally get to the closing table. If you want to survive that process and walk away with your number, you can't think of it as a quick skirmish.

That's why I use the terrorist analogy. The smart ones spend months or even years preparing for an operation. They know exactly what they want, they plan every angle, and then they execute relentlessly. Selling your business requires the same mindset: patience, persistence, and planning.

Never Give Without Getting

One of the principles I live by in negotiation is simple: *never give without getting something in return.*

Let's say the buyer uncovers a potential risk during due diligence. They ask for an additional rep and warranty. Maybe it's something relatively minor that's easy for you to provide. My advice? Don't just hand it over. Frame it like this: *"I'll give this to you today, but we both understand that down the road, when I need something, you'll return the favor. Agreed?"*

Even if what you get in exchange is just a goodwill chip you can use later, that's valuable. Because when negotiations stretch out—and they always do—you'll be glad you have those chips to cash in.

Creating Tension at the Table

A simple and effective way to negotiate from a position of strength is to have more than one buyer lined up. I love it when we've got a strong financial buyer and a strong strategic buyer at the table because their motivations are entirely different, and that creates tension. That tension gives you leverage, not just for price, but for better deal terms. It also gives you peace of mind as a seller. If one buyer tries to push too hard, you've got the option to walk away and take the backup offer. That changes the dynamic. The buyer knows they're not the only game in town.

I tell sellers all the time: it's my job to run the transaction; it's your job to run the business. Please don't get caught up in the back-and-forth I'm managing. Keep your foot on the gas with sales. Run leaner than you ever have before. Collect receivables faster than ever. Show buyers that not only is your company strong, but it's moving in the right direction—and fast. That's how you create real fear of missing out for buyers, and it's one of the most powerful negotiation tools you've got.

Price vs. Value

Here's something I remind sellers constantly: *price is what you pay, value is what you get.*

For the buyer, the price is the dollars leaving their pocket. Value is the business they're getting in return. For you, the seller, the price is the check you're taking home. Value is everything you've built that you're handing over.

Part of your M&A advisor's role is to set clear expectations about both—long before you ever go to market. I won't take a business to market until we're crystal clear on the valuation range, terms, and potential transition period.

I'll talk you through things like:

- The valuation range—what I believe is realistic and why.
- How long you'll probably need to stay on for transition, based on the size of your company and your industry.
- The likelihood of a seller's note and what those terms might look like.
- Working capital pegs—so you're not blindsided later by having to leave money in the business at closing.

By having these conversations upfront, you're not shocked when an LOI shows up with terms you've never heard of before.

Managing Both Sides of the Table

I spend just as much time managing buyer expectations. Before they submit an LOI, I'll ask them: *"What are you thinking? Let's talk it through."* If they're nowhere near the right ballpark, I'd rather know that upfront than waste everyone's time.

I also push buyers to do their homework: *"Have you done enough due diligence to be confident you won't have to retrade this deal?"* If the answer is no, I'd like to know what additional information they require from me to move forward.

At the same time, I'm upfront with sellers: retrades happen. Circumstances change, numbers can shift, and buyers will sometimes come back to adjust the deal. My job is to minimize that risk, but if it happens, you'll need to decide whether the deal is still worth moving forward.

Gutsy vs. Reckless

So how do you know when to hold the line and when to concede? That's the art of negotiation. Sometimes, standing firm on price makes sense because you've got the leverage, the performance numbers, and the buyer's motivation on your side. Other times, giving a concession is the smarter play if it keeps the deal alive and gets you closer to closing on favorable terms.

The difference between gutsy and reckless is knowing when to push and when to pivot. That's where experience matters and why you want someone at the table who is a skilled negotiator.

The Hidden Levers Sellers Don't Realize They Have

Most owners don't recognize how much control they have over the value of their business, especially when it comes to reducing perceived risk for buyers. Remember, price is always tied to risk. The lower the buyer perceives the risk, the more they're willing to pay.

Here are some of the biggest levers you can pull:

1. Make Recurring Revenue Truly Recurring

If you have customers paying you month after month, ensure those contracts are locked down in writing. Don't just rely on handshakes or verbal commitments. Implement multi-year contracts that automatically renew and include scheduled price increases so the buyer knows they're stepping into a business with predictable, growing revenue streams.

And don't forget to address *assignability* and *change-of-control* provisions. If those clauses aren't in your contracts, the buyer might have to renegotiate everything after the sale, which creates risk and drags down your value. Fix it before you go to market.

2. Multi-Thread Your Key Accounts

Take a look at your top five or ten customers. If only one person in your company manages each relationship—especially if that person is you—you've got a problem. Buyers hate concentration risk.

Instead, make sure every major account has at least two points of contact. And one of those contacts should be a non-family employee. That way, the customer sees the company—not just you—as their partner. This is especially critical when you've been the primary point of contact as the owner.

3. Clean Up and Defend Your Sales Pipeline

Don't show up with a messy sales report or a pile of leads you can't explain. Buyers want to see a pipeline that's clear, clean, and defensible.

Document your deals in progress. Show which proposals are out, which contracts are pending, and what purchase orders are expected in the next 30, 60, 90, or 120 days—whatever fits your sales cycle. That pipeline tells the buyer where you're headed, not just where you've been.

Every one of these moves reduces the fear a buyer has about the future of your company once you're gone. When they see locked-in contracts, multi-threaded relationships, and a solid sales pipeline, they stop worrying about what could go wrong and start focusing on how valuable your business is.

The Top 5 Buyer Negotiation Tricks and How to Flip Them

I could write an entire book on the tricks buyers use—and maybe someday I will. For now, here are the top five I see over and over again, and how to flip them back to your advantage.

1. Post-LOI Nibbles

This one drives me nuts. After the Letter of Intent (LOI) is signed, the buyer starts asking for little concessions—extra reps, warranties, small changes. At first, they seem harmless, but add them up, and suddenly you've given away a ton of value.

How to flip it: Every nibble has a price. If a buyer asks for an additional warranty, fine—but we adjust the earn-out in your favor. The lesson is simple: nothing is free.

2. Running Down the Clock

Some buyers deliberately drag out the process, hoping you'll get fatigued and give in. Big companies love this trick because they know time kills all deals.

How to flip it: Set hard deadlines in the LOI. Watch the "no shop" provision like a hawk—don't let it automatically renew forever. Trim extensions down from 30 days to 15. Continue to show the buyer that other parties are still interested. In one deal, 42 companies came to me after the LOI was signed, wanting to buy the business. Don't you think the buyer felt that pressure? Knowing the seller had options kept them honest.

3. The Lone-Horse Illusion

Buyers love to act like they're the only game in town. If you've only got one interested party, they'll squeeze you harder.

How to flip it: Create competition. Line up both strategic and financial buyers, as their motivations differ. That tension works in your favor.

4. The Last-Minute Discovery

Right before closing, the buyer "uncovers" some supposed new issue and tries to use it to retrade the deal. Nine times out of ten, it's nonsense.

How to flip it: Keep a clean, up-to-date data room. Document everything. That way, when they pull the stunt, you can say: "That's been in the data room for weeks. We discussed it five weeks ago. This is not new." Suddenly, their excuse to retrade collapses.

5. Death by a Thousand Cuts

Instead of one big retrade, the buyer chips away at your valuation by amplifying every tiny imperfection—operational, legal, or financial. The goal is the same: whittle you down until you cave.

How to flip it: Transparency. Build a strong pitch book upfront that highlights the good and also acknowledges the warts. If you disclose issues before the LOI, you can later say: "We told you that was there. You knew about it. No retrade."

The Power of Silence

Silence is one of the most underrated tools in negotiation. It doesn't damage trust—it builds leverage. The problem is, too many business owners, CPAs, and even lawyers don't know when to stop talking.

When you throw out your asking price or state a key term, stop. Don't immediately follow it with, *"But we can be flexible."* Let the buyer digest it. Let their team think about it. That pause creates leverage.

I had a deal recently where we received a very strong LOI. I sat on it for ten days without responding. Finally, the buyer emailed me saying, *"We haven't heard from you. Just know this isn't our final offer."* I laughed. They had just told me they were willing to sweeten the deal—and sure enough, I negotiated additional purchase price and better terms for my client simply by staying quiet.

Walking Away (The Right Way)

Now, unlike a terrorist, I don't believe in ultimatums. "Take it or leave it" is toxic. It damages trust, it fuels hostility, and it's almost impossible to walk back from.

Instead, I'll say something like, *"Maybe this structure doesn't work right now. Can you think about some other structures that might meet our shared goals, and then we can reconvene?"* It creates space without burning the bridge.

Every seller needs to know their walk-away point—on price, on earnouts, on payment timing, on transition period. Flexibility is necessary, but flexibility doesn't mean you have to be Gumby. If the terms get too far out of balance, it's better to pause, regroup, and let the other side come back with something closer to fair.

How to Know When a Buyer Really Wants the Deal

Negotiation is psychology as much as it is numbers. Half my job is what I jokingly call *M&A psychotherapy,* and not just with the seller. It's with the buyer, too.

When a buyer wants a deal, they'll start dropping clues. Here are three of the biggest ones I look for:

- **They shift from "if" to "when."** Early on, they'll say, *"If we get the business, we're thinking about…"* But when they're serious, it becomes, *"When we take over, we'll do…"* That's a huge tell.
- **They start solving problems instead of spotting them.** At first, buyers love pointing out every flaw. But when they want the deal, they shift gears. Their team of professionals stops raising roadblocks and starts working on solutions to get everyone to closing.
- **They accelerate communication.** Buyers know time kills all deals. If they really want it, they'll push for faster updates, quicker meetings, and shorter turnaround times.

Pay attention to those signals. They'll tell you more about your leverage than anything that comes out of the buyer's mouth.

Hardball Isn't Your Job

Too many owners think they have to go toe-to-toe with buyers. That's a mistake. Remember, you'll likely be working with this buyer for a transition period—sometimes six months, a year, or more. The last thing you want is a bitter taste in their mouth about how the deal got done.

Let your M&A advisor be the one they don't like. That's fine—we helicopter into the deal, do our jobs, get it closed, and then we're gone. You're the one left to work with the buyer. You need a cooperative relationship, not a hostile one.

I'd much rather see you and the buyer singing "Kumbaya" around the fire pit after closing, instead of fighting through lawyers during the transition. That's what rewards you with a smooth handoff, protects your legacy, and keeps the buyer motivated to make the business thrive.

Negotiating like a terrorist doesn't mean being ruthless or destructive. It means being strategic, relentless, and unwilling to accept no for an answer when yes is still on the table. It means creating tension, not hostility. It means never giving without getting. It means spotting the tricks buyers love to play and flipping them back in your favor.

It also means knowing when silence speaks louder than words, when to push, when to pause, and when to walk away. And most of all, it means having someone in your corner who can fight the hard battles while you keep building, keep performing, and keep your eyes on the prize: selling your business on the best terms possible so you can finally hit your number and enjoy the retirement you've earned.

KEY TAKEAWAYS

- Negotiating like a "terrorist" means being strategic, relentless, and knowing who holds the power to say yes—never taking the first no as final.
- The seller's job is to keep running and growing the business while the M&A advisor creates deal tension, manages buyers, and drives the negotiation forward.

- Never give without getting. Every concession should earn you goodwill or deal advantages to use later in the process.

- Reducing perceived risk through recurring contracts, multi-threaded relationships, and a clean sales pipeline is the fastest way to drive up valuation.

- The most competent negotiators create leverage through silence, structure walk-aways without hostility, and let their advisors play hardball so they can maintain a smooth post-sale transition.

CHAPTER FIVE

MAKE YOURSELF REPLACEABLE

B ack when I was running my company, EthiCare Advisors, I learned a valuable lesson that completely changed how I viewed being an owner.

I was on the golf course one afternoon with a friend—let's call him Mike B. Mike owned a company that was easily ten, maybe fifteen times the size of mine. We're talking a massive operation compared to what I had built at that time.

My phone was blowing up during the entire outing. Nonstop text messages, emails, calls from staff, calls from customers. That was just a normal day for me. Meanwhile, Mike's phone? Silent. Not a single buzz, ring, or alert the entire afternoon. He didn't check his email. He didn't get pulled into drama. Nothing.

Finally, I couldn't take it anymore. I asked him, "How can you do it?"

His answer was simple: *"You have to have the right team. If you can't take an afternoon off and play golf with a friend, you don't have the right team."*

At the time, I was in my early 30s, feeling invincible, and honestly, I thought I knew everything. But in that instant, I realized that I didn't have the right people in the right seats. My business was built around me being at the center of it all. And if I had been taken out of the picture—by a disability, an accident, or worse—my company may not have survived. At best, it would have been greatly diminished.

Here's the moral of the story: you have to build a business that doesn't depend on you. In fact, the goal should be to make yourself useless in the day-to-day.

I know that drives a lot of business owners crazy. Most owners want to be the center of the business. They like being the one everyone calls. They like being needed by their customers, vendors, and employees. The reality is that when the business depends on you, it's worth less. That kind of dependency makes your company harder to sell. It forces buyers to see more risk. And it usually means you'll be stuck around longer—maybe with a lengthy transition period, maybe with an earn-out tied to performance.

If you want top dollar for your business, you need to make it owner-independent. That should be the goal of every owner out there.

Getting Out of the Weeds Without Losing Control

You're probably thinking: *"If I step back, won't everything fall apart?"*

I used to think the same way. I felt I had to be in the weeds because that's where my "secret sauce" lived—the special touch that made the company attractive to customers. But that thinking is precisely what creates an owner dependency problem.

You *can* begin to remove yourself without losing control. The way you do it is by building, mentoring, and leading the best team possible. Steve Jobs once said, *"It doesn't make sense to hire smart people and tell them what to do. We (Apple) hire smart people so they can tell us what to do."*

That took me a long time to understand. However, once I hired people who actually knew more about medical claims and insurance than I did, the company reached a whole new level.

If you want to stop getting pulled back into the daily chaos, you need to:

- Hire smart people.
- Train and mentor them well.
- Lead them with clear expectations.

And then—this part is critical—you hold them accountable with systems. Standard Operating Procedures (SOPs), tied to Key Performance Indicators (KPIs), and monitored through an owner dashboard. That's how you manage the weeds without being *in* the weeds.

Practical Steps That Work

So, what does this look like in practice? I'll break it down into two areas: sales and service (or product) delivery.

1. Sales

If you want your business to run smoothly without you, the first thing you need to do is stop being the primary point of contact for customers. Ideally, your customers shouldn't even know your name.

That might sound extreme, and depending on your industry, it may not be 100% realistic. But it's something to shoot for. Because when a buyer asks, *"What are your top ten client relationships like with the owner?"*—the best possible answer is, *"They don't even know who I am."*

One way to make this work is to put two employees on every account. That way, customers always know at least two people within the company who can assist them. If one employee leaves, there's no disruption—the account has continuity.

2. Service and Product Delivery

The same goes for your service or product delivery. The owner should not be the one doing the work. If your business only runs well when you're the one delivering, it's not ready to sell.

Your team needs to handle the work, so it doesn't matter whether you're in your office, on a cruise, or touring Europe—the customer experience stays the same.

That's where SOPs really shine. Document your processes. Ensure delivery is consistent, regardless of which team member is involved. That way, new people can be trained quickly, employees can be held accountable, and customers can be assured that they'll always receive the same level of service.

When customers can't tell whether they're working with you, Mary, Tom, or anyone else on your team, you've built a company that's scalable, sellable, and truly valuable.

The Kidnap Test

One of my favorite ways to get business owners thinking about owner dependency is to run them through what I call the *Kidnap Test*.

I'll ask: *"If I kidnapped you today and brought you back tomorrow, how much would that impact your business?"*

Most owners say, *"Not much. We'd be fine."*

Then I up the stakes. *"What if I kidnapped you today and didn't return you for seven days?"* In a perfect world, the answer should still be: *"Not at all."*

Then I stretch it further: *"What about two weeks? What about a month? What would happen then? Where would the cracks show?"*

This isn't about kidnappings, of course—it's about continuity. What if you were temporarily disabled? What if you had to attend to a family medical emergency? Could your business run without you? Or would things start to unravel?

Succession planning is good business planning. The sooner you start thinking about it, the stronger your company will be. This varies by industry, but in most cases, having a number two is a smart approach to succession planning. It gives you someone you can delegate to. Someone you can trust to answer questions and make decisions. Someone empowered to keep the company running, so not every issue falls on your lap.

In some industries, this is even more important. Take electrical contractors, for example. Usually, the owner is the license holder. That creates a huge problem if the owner ever wants—or needs—to step away. If the owner gets sick, retires, or worse, dies, the business is at risk. But if that company has a licensed number two, suddenly the whole picture changes.

Recruiting and retaining a strong second-in-command may cost more money upfront, but it's one of the wisest investments you can make. It makes your life easier day-to-day and can also exponentially increase the value of your business when it comes time to sell.

When Owner Dependency Costs
You at the Closing Table

If your business can't run without you, buyers will notice, and you'll pay for it.

One of the first ways this is evident is through an *earn-out*. Earn-outs are tools buyers use to de-risk their purchase when the owner's involvement is mission-critical. If you're the top sales guy, or you're the only person with the specialized know-how to deliver your product or service, the buyer isn't going to cut you a big check on day one and walk away happy. They're going to say, *"I'll pay you X dollars at closing, and then you'll have the chance to earn an additional Y dollars if the company hits certain targets over the next 12–36 months."*

Sounds fine in theory, but here's my rule: Don't bank on the earn-out. Many times, sellers never see that money. Buyers use earn-outs to shift risk back onto you.

Another scenario I often see is when the owner is actually doing two jobs. Maybe you're working 60 hours a week, covering multiple roles, but when a buyer steps in, they can't do that. They'll need to hire someone—maybe two people—to replace what you were doing.

When we recast financials to calculate your Seller's Discretionary Earnings (SDE), we adjust for things that benefit you as the owner but wouldn't necessarily carry over to a new owner. These adjustments are called add-backs.

For example, let's say you're taking $300,000 in salary, but part of that represents you doing multiple jobs. If a new owner had to hire someone else to cover that work, then part of that $300,000 isn't really discretionary—it's an expense the business must cover. So instead of $300,000 flowing through as SDE, maybe only $200,000 counts after adjusting for a replacement salary. That change alone could reduce your valuation by as much as a third. That's a huge hit, and it's completely avoidable if you start pulling yourself out a few years in advance.

The First Step You Can Take Tomorrow

If you're reading this thinking, *"Nothing runs without me,"* let me challenge you with one soul-searching question:

Is it that you don't have confidence in your employees?

If the honest answer is no—if you don't trust your people—then you don't have the right people. It's that simple. And that means your first step is to train and mentor your existing team, or go out and find new employees who can carry the weight.

But if the answer is yes—if you really do trust your people—then the problem isn't them. It's you. It's in your head. In that case, the first step you need to take tomorrow is to get out of their way and let them do the job you hired them to do.

Always put yourself in the buyer's shoes. If you were looking to buy a business and saw that the owner was wearing three hats, working 60 hours a week, and acting as chief cook and bottle washer, what would you think? You'd see risk. You'd see yourself stepping into a job, not a business. And you'd lower your offer to reflect that.

Now imagine the opposite. You walk in and see that the owner only works an hour or two a day. The company runs on a strong management team, a solid sales team, and a reliable operations crew. As a buyer, that gives you confidence. That makes you want to pay a premium, not negotiate down.

Buyers aren't looking to buy jobs. They're looking to buy revenue that turns into profits. Strategic buyers are seeking to acquire market share. Financial buyers are looking for a platform they can scale with more acquisitions. In both cases, they want stability, predictability, and growth potential.

So ask yourself the tough questions. Put your business through the Kidnap Test. Invest in your team. Build management depth. Document your systems. Remove yourself from the center of it all. Because when you do, you create a business that's both easier to sell and worthy of top dollar.

HOW DEPENDENT IS YOUR BUSINESS ON YOU? SCORE YOURSELF HONESTLY.

Instructions: Rate each statement below from **1 (Not true at all)** to **5 (Completely true)**. Add up your points at the end.

Section 1: Day-to-Day Operations

1. Clients expect to deal with me personally.
2. I am the primary decision-maker for daily issues.
3. If I'm out for more than a week, the business stalls.

Section 2: People & Management

4. No clear second-in-command or leadership team can run the business without me.
5. Employees frequently ask me for direction instead of making decisions.
6. Key relationships (suppliers, partners, bankers) rely solely on me.

Section 3: Sales & Growth

7. Most new business comes directly from my personal efforts.
8. Customers associate the brand more with me than the company itself.
9. Without me, marketing and sales activity would decline sharply.

Section 4: Systems & Processes

10. We don't have written SOPs (Standard Operating Procedures).
11. Knowledge of how things "really get done" lives mostly in my head.
12. Technology and reporting systems are not strong enough to operate without me monitoring them.

Scoring

- **45–60 points: 🔒 High Dependency.** Your business IS you. Is it a job or is it a business? This will scare buyers and lower value. Time to take action.
- **30–44 points: ⚠ Moderate Dependency.** Some structure exists, but you're still too central. Improvements here could significantly increase value.
- **15–29 points: ✅ Low Dependency.** Congratulations—you're largely replaceable. Buyers will pay a premium for this.

Next Step:

Pick ONE area where your score was the highest and commit to reducing dependency there first. Over time, replacing yourself in these areas will not only make your business more valuable— it will make your life easier, too.

KEY TAKEAWAYS

- The more your business depends on you, the less valuable and harder it becomes to sell.
- Building a strong, well-trained, and accountable team is essential to stepping out of the weeds without losing control.
- Buyers want to purchase systems, not personalities—so stop being the face of your business and make your operations replicable.
- Tools like SOPs, KPIs, dashboards, and a second-in-command create continuity, reduce risk, and increase valuation.
- Start by identifying where you're most essential, then take action to replace yourself in that area first.

CHAPTER SIX
DON'T TRUST YOUR COUSIN VINNY

P icture this. You're about to sell your business — the biggest financial moment of your life. The conference room is full of seasoned attorneys who've negotiated hundreds of deals. And then through the door walks your lawyer: Cousin Vinny—leather jacket, thick accent, no M&A experience whatsoever. Your retirement, your legacy, and your family's future are all riding on someone who's in way over their head.

I'm based in New Jersey, and here, business brokers aren't regulated like realtors. In some states, they are, but not here. So let's say your nephew Freddie is a realtor. Great kid, friendly enough. But does that make him a Certified Business Intermediary (CBI)? Has he been adequately trained on how to guide you through the *entire* process of selling a business? The answer is probably not. And just because Freddie would love to earn a commission when you sell doesn't mean you should hand over the sale of your life's work to him. Selling a business is not the same as selling a three-bedroom colonial. You can't afford to gamble your retirement on someone who's learning as they go.

Maybe Auntie Bobby has been your bookkeeper forever. She does a fantastic job sending out invoices, making collections, and calling in payroll. But when it comes to recasting financials — digging in to capture every last bit of seller's discretionary earnings — she's out of her depth. That's not her fault; it's not her training. You need an expert who knows how to take Auntie Bobby's work and elevate it to the level buyers expect when they scrutinize your books.

And, of course, we can't forget Cousin Vinny. Maybe he's a divorce attorney, or perhaps you remember him from Hollywood as the inexperienced lawyer whose very first case involved "the two yutes." That might make for a funny movie, but in real life, you don't want to pay a lawyer to learn M&A on your dime. You want a transaction attorney who has lived and breathed business deals, not one who's better at dividing up furniture in a divorce. You only sell your business once. Please don't make it a training exercise for somebody else's résumé.

The wrong advisor can cost you hundreds of thousands, even millions. The right ones, though, will earn you far more than they cost by getting your deal done clean, fast, and profitable.

It's Not Just About Your Side of the Table

Something most sellers don't think about is that advisors matter on both sides of the transaction. When you're evaluating a buyer, don't be afraid to ask your advisor, *Who's representing them? Who's their attorney, and what experience do they bring? Who's their CPA, and how many deals have they been through?*

If the buyer's advisors are inexperienced, the whole process can get bogged down, dragged out, or even blown up completely. I can't tell you how many deals get derailed not because the buyer or seller didn't want to do it, but because someone on the advisory team didn't know what they were doing.

The Trap of Too Many Voices

Another mistake I see is owners relying too heavily on multiple people for advice. It's like that old saying: ask three lawyers for an opinion and you'll get five opinions. Instead of focusing on their deal team, owners start listening to everyone with a pulse. Nephew Freddie has ideas. Auntie Bobby has concerns. Cousin Vinny has opinions. And then there's the endless "locker room talk" from the country club. I call it Country Club Locker Room Head Trash — the nonsense you pick up from golf buddies who brag about how their sale went or how much they got.

Every transaction is different. Every deal takes on a life of its own. Sure, there are lessons to be learned from others, but your situation is unique. If you try to build your strategy out of secondhand stories and scattered opinions, you'll confuse yourself, waste time, and maybe even tank the entire sale.

The smartest move you can make is to hire the best CPA, the best transaction attorney, and the best M&A advisor you can find. Make them your advisory board. Then rely on them — not the peanut gallery — to get you across the finish line.

Building Your Dream Team

Who should actually be on your dream team of advisors? Let's start backwards. If you're a smart owner doing this the right way, you'll already have an exit planner involved several years out. That exit planner should work hand-in-hand with your wealth manager or financial advisor to make sure there's a clear plan in place.

When the business sells, you need to know you're walking away with the money you require for the next stage of your life. Maybe that's retirement. Perhaps it's buying another business in a totally different industry. Maybe it's something else entirely. Whatever it is, your financial team should help set you up so the sale funds your future.

When you're actually ready to list the business and go to market, the next layer of your team comes in. You'll need:

- A mergers and acquisitions advisor (sometimes still called a business broker in the lower middle market)
- A transaction attorney
- A CPA with real transaction experience

The best time to build this team is a couple of years in advance. That gives you time to establish relationships and prepare for the complexity of your particular deal. Every industry is different, and the size and nature of your business matter. But one to two years out is common. That's when owners often call me for a valuation — not necessarily to sell right away, but to find out what their business is worth and to start planning.

From there, I stay in touch, providing updates and education so that by the time they're truly ready to list, they've already got a much better understanding of the process. They're prepared, confident, and surrounded by people who know exactly how to get things done.

The ROI of Hiring the Right Advisors

One of the first objections I hear from owners is about cost. *"Mark, do I really need to hire the top advisors? Aren't they expensive?"*

Hiring top advisors doesn't mean paying an arm and a leg. Fees are often negotiable. And yes, you could cut corners and hire someone less experienced for a lower hourly rate. But then we are right back to Cousin Vinny. If you're paying Vinny to learn on the job, your deal is going to take longer, negotiations will drag, and you'll bleed money while he tries to figure out what's commercially acceptable in a transaction and what isn't. The longer things take, the more it costs you.

The right professionals actually save you money. They know the shortcuts, they know the landmines, and they can get you to the closing table without wasting months of your life (and thousands of your dollars). Hiring the right advisors almost always delivers a positive ROI.

What Advisors Charge

Here is a quick breakdown of how these advisors typically bill.

- **CPAs and Transaction Attorneys:** Generally charge an hourly rate. The difference between a generalist attorney and a good transaction attorney usually isn't much. But the *value* difference is massive, because the transaction specialist will save you time, and time equals money.
- **Exit Planners:** Usually charge on a project basis. They'll build you an exit plan, sometimes with quarterly coaching sessions, depending on your needs.
- **M&A Brokers / Advisors:** Typically, there's a monthly retainer — anywhere from a thousand to a few thousand dollars, sometimes more. In addition, there's a success fee when the deal closes. Some retainers are credited back against the success fee, depending on the agreement. Success fees are often based on the double Lehman scale, which is the current market standard. In some cases, I've even structured deals on an hourly basis, though that's less common.
- **Valuations:** A solid business valuation as a starting point can range anywhere from $5,000 to $20,000, depending on the complexity of the business and the scope of the analysis.

When you add it all up, these numbers pale in comparison to the cost of a botched deal or money left on the table.

The High Price of Bad Advice

I was at a networking event at my country club, chatting with a financial advisor. I asked him, *"Do you work with a lot of business owners?"* He said yes. So I followed up, *"Okay, when you're building financial plans for them, how do you value their businesses?"*

He looked me dead in the eye and said, *"Oh, that's real simple. If the business does more than a million in sales, I take three times what the owner puts in their pocket. If it's under a million, I use two times."*

I said, *"You don't use any comp data? You don't tap into any valuation databases?"* His answer? *"Nah, that's not worth it."*

That kind of thinking is dangerous. Sure, those back-of-the-napkin multiples are half a decent rule of thumb, but they're also half garbage. They don't take into account industry comps, market conditions, growth potential, or the improvements you can make before selling. For something as serious as a financial plan — or worse, a sale — you need a proper valuation.

A qualified M&A advisor doesn't just slap a multiple on earnings. They dig in. They identify the fundamental value drivers in your business, the things you can work on now to make it worth more later. That's the difference between a plan that sets you up for retirement and one that sets you up for disappointment.

How do you know if an advisor truly understands M&A versus one who's just along for the ride?

Look for battle scars. Business owners choose to work with me because I've been where they are. I built a business. I dealt with the chaos of a startup. I hired and fired. I weathered the boom and bust cycles, including the mess around Obamacare in the industry I was in. And then I exited for eight figures.

I know what it's like to carry the weight of payroll. I know what it's like to sweat the numbers and worry about the future. When you're building your team, find advisors who *get it*—people who've lived the ups and downs and who understand what's at stake.

You have probably built long-term relationships with your current advisors, and rightfully so. Your CPA, your attorney, your banker — they've helped you get here. They've been in the trenches with you. But just because they got you this far doesn't mean they're the ones who can get you across the finish line when it comes to selling your business.

You don't need to fire them. In fact, depending on the size of their firm, there may be other specialists under the same roof. Do a little research. Go to the website. Don't be afraid to say, *"Hey, I see Mary at your firm specializes in transactions. Could you introduce us? Maybe the three of us can grab lunch and talk about how Mary can help as I move into selling the company."* Most good advisors will support you in bringing in the right person.

Here's how I think about it. I have an amazing primary care doctor. Great guy. Smart. Trustworthy. But if I had a brain tumor, there's no way I'd let him do the surgery. He'd refer me to the best brain surgeon he could find, and he'd insist on it. Not all doctors are brain surgeons. Not all CPAs or attorneys specialize in transactions.

This is the biggest financial event of your life. Don't hand it off to Cousin Vinny, Auntie Bobby, or nephew Freddie just because they're familiar faces. Loyalty is admirable. But when it comes to your legacy, you need more than loyalty. You need expertise. Surround yourself with the right team, lean on them, and make this exit the one that counts.

KEY TAKEAWAYS

- Don't gamble your future on familiar faces—your cousin, your bookkeeper, and your real estate agent aren't qualified to handle the most significant transaction of your life. You need actual M&A expertise.
- Every advisor on the buyer *and* seller side matters. Inexperience on either end can drag out or derail a deal altogether.
- Avoid "Country Club Locker Room Head Trash." Stick to the advisors you've carefully selected instead of listening to scattered opinions and stories from people who haven't walked in your shoes.
- Start building your advisory team—exit planner, financial advisor, M&A broker, transaction attorney, and CPA—at least one to two years before you plan to sell so that they can guide you with clarity and confidence.
- Hiring the right advisors costs money, but not hiring them can cost you far more. Expertise pays for itself through faster closings, stronger valuations, and fewer costly mistakes.

CHAPTER SEVEN

THE LAST 100 DAYS: WHAT HAPPENS BETWEEN LOI AND WIRE TRANSFER

I call this part of the journey *the yellow light of closings*. It's where the rubber meets the road. Everything either comes together beautifully, or it doesn't go right at all. I've witnessed both extremes. On one side, you've got the wonderful, spectacular "rainbows, unicorns, and lollipops" type of deal—everybody singing "Kumbaya" around the closing table, smiling and shaking hands. On the other side, there are deals that just flat-out blow up and never make it there.

Why is there such a wide gap in outcomes? Because these last 100 days are wildly emotional and stressful—for you as the seller, for the buyer, and even for all the advisors around the table.

Buyers have a laundry list of "to-dos," especially when outside money is involved. If the deal requires SBA funding, investor money, or private equity dollars, you can bet their side is buried in paperwork. Every box has to be checked. Every document has to be verified. They're under the gun to justify every penny they're putting on the table.

For sellers, the stress often feels very personal. You'll feel like you're being asked the same question seven ways from Sunday. You'll feel like your business practices are being put on trial. Every decision you made, every system you've built, every detail of your financials—it all gets challenged, not necessarily in a bad way, but in a relentless way. And that can wear you down.

If you think the first 100 days of "the dance"—courting buyers, negotiating terms, and landing a letter of intent—were tough, wait. The last 100 days might be even more stressful. This is where the transaction actually lives or dies. The promises of the LOI either turn into a wire transfer hitting your account or a deal that crashes before you ever get to the table.

Don't Sabotage Your Own Deal

One of the biggest risks in these last 100 days isn't the buyer, the bank, or the lawyers—it's you. Sellers sabotage their own deals more often than you'd think, and it usually happens because they don't stay in their own lane.

Your lane is simple: keep running your business like it's not for sale. Go land a new client. Get an existing client to give you more work. Keep your employees engaged and happy. Freshen up your website. Post consistently on social media. Do the things that make your business look wildly attractive and "sexy" to a buyer. Deals can fall apart if your business stumbles during due diligence. Buyers watch sales and profits like hawks in this stage. If you miss a month, or worse, miss a quarter, it gives them the perfect excuse to "retrade" the deal—meaning they'll try to lower the price or change the terms.

Retrading is one of those words that makes every seller's stomach drop. It's when a buyer tries to adjust the price or terms after the LOI is signed, usually during due diligence. Sometimes it's legitimate, and sometimes it's just a game.

Here's the difference. If your sales dip or if profits take a hit during the process, that opens the door for a legitimate retrade. The buyer isn't wrong to say, "Hey, this business isn't performing the way we expected when we made the offer." That's why I keep hammering on the point: don't miss the quarter, don't miss the month. Maintain steady performance throughout the closing process.

Now, if you blow it out of the park—if sales skyrocket during diligence—don't expect to get a higher price out of the buyer. It doesn't work both ways. What you can expect is to gain leverage on other terms of the deal. Perhaps you can negotiate a better earnout structure or secure more favorable transition terms. So outperforming helps, but it won't change the headline number.

Bad faith retrading is a whole different animal. That's when you've already supplied information—maybe it was on page four of your confidential information memorandum or sitting in the dataroom for 90 days—and the buyer suddenly pretends it's "new" and uses it as an excuse to chip away at the price. At that point, it's not about the numbers; it's about tactics. Either the buyer's due diligence was sloppy, or they're just playing games.

And that's where documentation becomes critical. If we can point to the fact that we disclosed it up front, then we know it's not a legitimate issue—it's a buyer trying to get cute. That's when you need an advisor in your corner who can call it out for what it is and protect the value you worked so hard to build.

Your M&A advisor's role is to run the deal, including negotiating terms, managing due diligence, and coordinating with attorneys and accountants. Most business owners don't get a do-over. You build, you work, you grow—and when the time comes to retire, you sell. That's it. Don't let stress or curiosity push you into second-guessing your advisors or micromanaging the process. Have faith in your team to do what they're good at, and you keep doing what you're good at.

In God We Trust, Everyone Else... Prepare for Due Diligence

When I walk a first-time seller into this process, I give them my standard line: *"In God we trust, everyone else... prepare for due diligence."*

It's not personal—it's just trust but verify. Every claim you make, every number on your financials, every contract—you should expect the buyer to want verification. That's what you would do if you were the one writing the check. I'll often flip the perspective and ask: *If you were buying this business, what kind of due diligence would you want to see?* That usually helps sellers realize due diligence is fair, even if it feels invasive.

If a buyer pushes too hard or gets unreasonable, your advisor can act as the referee, step in and say, "That's not commercially reasonable," or "Here's the documentation you need—it's already in the dataroom." Having someone to set boundaries makes all the difference. Sellers need to know they've got someone in their corner keeping things fair and on track.

Due diligence is no seller's favorite part. It's tough. This is the phase where it feels like every decision you've ever made about your business over the past twenty or thirty years is suddenly being second-guessed. That perception—that every choice was "wrong" in the eyes of the buyer—is what I call head trash. It's not that the buyer thinks you're a bad operator. It's that they're looking at the business through the lens of *how they'll run it in the future.* They may change certain practices.

They may reorganize the team. They may tweak products or services. None of that means what you built wasn't successful. It simply means they want to shape the company into something that fits their vision going forward.

If you get hung up on feeling challenged, you'll drive yourself crazy. Keep your eyes on that outcome and let the noise roll off your back.

Keep the Ball Moving

The size of the transaction often dictates the intensity of due diligence, but one thing is true across the board: you need structure. In lower-middle-market transactions, especially, weekly meetings between the principals are absolutely critical.

In these last 100 days, there's always something to work through. One week, it might be legal issues that require the attorneys to be at the table. Another week, it might be environmental concerns, so the consultants need to weigh in. Sometimes it's tax or accounting, sometimes HR. No matter what it is, without a rhythm of weekly check-ins, the process drags and minor issues snowball into big problems.

To keep a deal on track, schedule recurring meetings on the calendar and ensure the right professionals are involved when their expertise is required.

Preparing Beyond the Paperwork

The part most sellers don't think about until it's too late is personal and family preparation. On paper, it looks easy. The seller agrees to give 100% for the last 100 days, pushing hard to keep the business strong, and then, after closing, they finally get to exhale. Maybe take a two-week vacation, celebrate, recharge.

However, remember that buyers don't want you to disappear right after closing. They need you present for the transition. Employees need reassurance that you're still there to guide them, even if it's only for a limited time. So while you might be dreaming about the beach, the buyer is expecting you in the office, making introductions, smoothing the handoff, and honoring the commitments in your transition agreement.

I tell every seller to work these things out early. Don't wait until after the wire hits to negotiate how much time you'll give the buyer, or when you can finally step away. The sooner you set those expectations—sometimes as early as the LOI—the smoother things go post-closing. Buyers, sellers, and employees should all know what to expect once the ink is dry.

Last-Minute Surprises

If there's one myth I wish I could put to rest, it's that every deal follows the same script. The truth is, every last 100 days takes on a life of its own. Yes, there are patterns and familiar steps, but no two transactions ever unfold exactly the same way.

I've seen it firsthand. In one scenario, everything was basically finished. Contracts were 99% done. Closing was just five days away. And then a working capital adjustment came up that created too big of a variance for the sellers to stomach and they walked.

You've got to anticipate surprises. They're not the exception—they're part of the process. And when they show up, it's the job of the advisors to coach both sides on how to move forward, if closing is really what everyone still wants.

Don't Sweat the Small Stuff

Looking back, the best piece of advice I can give any seller about surviving the last 100 days is this: don't sweat the small stuff. Every deal is going to have some hair on it. There's no such thing as a perfect transaction. Both buyer and seller are likely to encounter situations where they must ask: *Is this worth fighting for? Or is this something I can let go?*

The danger is getting caught up in a thousand tiny cuts—arguing over every little detail until the deal bleeds out. The key is to stay flexible and realistic. Focus on the big things that truly matter, and work hard to bridge the gap on those.

The last 100 days are where deals are won or lost—not just financially, but emotionally. This is the stretch where stress peaks, head trash creeps in, and surprises test everyone's patience. But it's also the sprint that gets you to the reward you've worked decades for. If you can stay in your lane, keep your business strong, trust your advisors, and maintain perspective when the small stuff arises, you give yourself the best chance of crossing the finish line.

KEY TAKEAWAYS

- The last 100 days are the "yellow light" of closing—emotional, stressful, and make-or-break for turning an LOI into a wire transfer.
- Sellers sabotage deals when they take their eye off the business; steady performance keeps buyers from retrading on price or terms.

- Due diligence is relentless but fair—buyers are verifying, not attacking, and strong documentation helps shut down bad-faith tactics.
- Weekly meetings with the right professionals keep the process moving and prevent small issues from snowballing.
- Expect surprises, stay flexible, and don't sweat the small stuff—focus on what truly matters to ensure a successful deal.

PART THREE

THE EXIT YOU DESERVE

CHAPTER EIGHT
YOUR SWEAT EQUITY PAYDAY

here's an old saying in mergers and acquisitions: there are only two ways to exit a business—vertically or horizontally. Now, of course, that's a bit of a joke, but it drives home a serious point. You either walk out the front door on your own two feet, or you're carried out because you've been hit with a disability or worse.

It's always better to plan for a vertical exit. That's when you're in control, and that's when you're going to get the biggest payday. If you wait too long—if health issues or death force your hand—buyers will smell blood in the water. And when they do, they'll use it to their advantage. They'll push harder, offer less, and you'll have no leverage left.

I don't want that for you. I want every business owner to get the outcome they deserve—the one that rewards all the years of hard work and sacrifice you've put into building your business. That's your sweat equity payday.

Please don't fall into the trap of thinking you're automatically entitled to it. It doesn't happen by accident. It takes planning. It takes time. And it takes a strong team—both within your business and outside advisors—to ensure you capture maximum value when you exit.

Why Selling Takes Longer Than You Think

A big surprise for many business owners is just how long it takes to get from a signed Letter of Intent (LOI) to the actual closing. On paper, it should be between 60 and 90 days. But I've seen it drag on much longer.

No two deals are ever the same. Every business is different, every buyer is different, and every transaction has its own moving parts. And while some delays are predictable, others sneak up and catch you off guard.

For example, in some states, there are regulatory hurdles you'd never even think about until you're in the middle of the process. In New Jersey, we have a law known as the Industrial Site Recovery Act. If you're selling a manufacturing business, you may need special approvals under that law before the deal can close. That can easily add weeks or months to the process without proper planning and the right professionals to help along the way.

In other industries, you may need customer approvals to transfer ownership. That's another step that takes time, and sometimes it introduces a risk if a customer decides they're not comfortable with the change. Then, of course, there are lender approvals—whether it's an SBA bank loan, a private equity group, or a family office. Financing always adds layers of review, and each layer is another opportunity for delay.

The key is setting realistic expectations from the start. Sellers often walk in thinking this will be a quick process, only to become frustrated when the calendar keeps stretching out. A good M&A advisor will help you navigate that—knowing when to be flexible and when to push hard to keep the timetable intact.

Expect the unexpected. Selling almost always takes longer than you think. If you go in prepared for that reality, you'll save yourself a lot of stress and frustration along the way.

When Walking Away Is the Right Move

Not every story ends with a signed deal and a wire transfer. Sometimes, the smartest and most confident decision an owner can make is to walk away.

I worked with a group of founders who got all the way to the finish line—we were five days from closing. At that point, the buyers started playing games with the working capital numbers, and what initially looked like a great deal quickly began to look like a raw deal. The founders had a choice: take what was on the table or walk.

Not only did they walk away from that particular buyer, but they also walked away from selling altogether. They chose instead to transition the business internally to the next generation of employees—some family, some not.

Because the buyer in this case was a division of a publicly traded company, the founders realized that their legacy, their brand, and the company's role in the community would eventually be absorbed, stripped down, and forgotten. To them, that wasn't worth it. That decision took guts. It also showed confidence. They believed the future of the company was stronger in the hands of the people who had built it alongside them, and they acted on that belief.

Knowing When It's the Right Deal

On the other hand, I've seen numerous successful exits where the owner walked away with money in the bank and a sense of peace of mind. Those deals happen every day.

You might have heard "the multiple means everything," and in many ways, it does. But it's not the only thing. When you're selling your business, the deal terms are just as important as the price. When do you actually get the money? Is part of it tied up in a seller note? Is there an earnout, and if so, how long is it going to drag on? What does the transition plan look like—are you expected to spend every Saturday for the next six months training the buyer? And what about family members who work in the business—what happens to them once you've signed on the dotted line?

Then there's the legal side. The asset purchase agreement or stock purchase agreement will be loaded with reps and warranties, and those matter just as much as the dollar figure. They can have major consequences for you post-sale if you're not paying attention.

And don't underestimate the emotional side of this either. Sellers' remorse is very real. I recently attended an event where I spoke with a roomful of business owners who had sold their companies. Every single one of them—10 out of 10—said they experienced some form of remorse. Some felt it right away, while others felt it months later, but it was always there. The best thing you can do is expect it and prepare for it.

So please think beyond the number. Make sure the terms, the structure, and the life you're walking into next are just as rewarding as the check you're cashing.

Before you sign on the dotted line, you need to pause and ask yourself a few questions:

- *Is this the best financial outcome I can realistically achieve right now?*

- *Am I satisfied with when and how I'll be paid?*
- *Do I understand how much transition will be required of me post-closing?*
- *What happens to family members or long-term employees in the business?*
- *How will this deal affect my brand, my legacy, and my reputation in the community?*
- *Do I have clarity about my next chapter in life?*

If you can look at all of that and still say, "Yes, I'm happy with this deal," then it's time to sign and close. If not, it's better to wait, regroup, or even walk away.

Celebrate–But Time It Right

If you do decide to sign and close, celebration is important, but timing is everything. Don't pop the champagne until the money actually hits your account. And even then, don't expect the party to last long.

Sellers are usually surprised to find that minutes after closing, the work is not yet over. The wire clears, and suddenly the buyer wants you to announce the deal to employees, call key customers, notify vendors, and start working on transition responsibilities. The buyers want to hit the ground running, foot on the gas pedal.

Meanwhile, the seller—understandably—is exhausted. After the sprint to the finish line, owners just want a break. They dream of a vacation, some time off, and a chance to exhale. That's healthy. That's normal. And it should be part of the negotiation.

So yes, you should celebrate. The milestone of selling a business deserves recognition, both for you and for the family and friends who supported you along the way. Just make sure you plan ahead for what that celebration looks like so it doesn't clash with the buyer's expectations post-closing.

Selling Isn't the End—It's the Reward

Most business owners I meet have sacrificed a lot more than people realize. You've skipped family suppers. You've missed soccer games. You've crisscrossed the country chasing vendors and customers, sleeping in uncomfortable beds at sketchy motels and hotels. You've eaten more Marriott burgers cooked like hockey pucks than you care to admit.

Sure, you got paid along the way. The business has supported your family and your lifestyle. But you can't put a price tag on missing time with your kids, or with your nieces and nephews, or the countless other family moments you never got back.

The real payday—the one that makes all those sacrifices worth it—comes at the end. It's when you sell the business and unlock the equity you've been building all these years. That's the reward.

What Comes After the Sale

So what's next? Some owners tell me they want to travel or play golf. That sounds nice, but unless you're buying a condo on a cruise ship and living at sea forever, you're only going to travel some of the time. And unless you've already been golfing five days a week, chances are you won't suddenly start after you sell.

Business owners are often Type A personalities. You've spent decades grinding, leading, and building. When that day-to-day work is gone, you need something else to fill the void. For some, it's volunteering with a local service club, their church, or a charity. For others, it might be mentoring younger entrepreneurs or serving on boards. Either way, you need a plan.

I can speak from personal experience here. When I sold EthiCare Advisors in 2017, my wife was on track to become a prominent leader in a nonprofit organization. I decided to step in and support her heavily. That experience helped fill a significant portion of the void that comes with selling a business. And as I later went on to grow my M&A firm, I realized how important that time was in helping me transition personally.

Think about your life post-sale. Think about what will keep you fulfilled for the next decade or two. That's what makes your sweat equity payday truly rewarding, and we will discuss this more in depth in the next chapter.

Your Three-Step Starting Point

If you're dreaming of your sweat equity payday, here's where to begin. Think of it like a three-legged stool:

- ★ **De-risk the business.** Reduce customer, vendor, and employee concentration. No single customer should make up too much of your revenue. No single vendor should hold you hostage. And no single employee—especially in a key role— should be the only person holding the keys to your largest account. And the biggest one of all? Owner dependence. The less your business relies on you personally, the more valuable it becomes.
- ★ **Tighten your financial reporting.** Get your books in order now—years before you plan to sell. Work with your CFO, controller, or bookkeeper internally, and make sure your

external accounting firm is preparing financials that will survive a buyer's due diligence. Clean numbers build confidence and increase value.

★ **Build your dream deal team.** Don't rely on cousin Vinny the lawyer or a CPA who's never touched a transaction your size. You need specialists: a seasoned transaction attorney, a CPA or accountant with M&A experience, and an M&A advisor who can quarterback the entire process. With the right team, the deal gets done smoother, faster, and with far less risk of leaving money on the table.

Focus on these three areas, and you'll not only increase your company's value— you'll give yourself the best shot at walking out the door vertically, on your own terms. That's the real sweat equity payday. And it's waiting for you—if you start planning today.

KEY TAKEAWAYS

- A sweat equity payday doesn't happen by accident. It requires planning, time, and the right advisory team to maximize value and control your exit.
- Selling almost always takes longer than expected, so set realistic expectations and prepare for delays.
- Walking away from a deal can sometimes be the smartest move if it protects your legacy, values, or long-term goals.
- The biggest payday isn't just about the number—deal terms, transition obligations, and your life after the sale matter just as much.
- De-risking your business, tightening financial reporting, and building a dream deal team are the three pillars that make your payday possible.

CHAPTER NINE
WHAT COMES NEXT?

S elling your business is a milestone. It's one of those big life moments like graduating from college, getting married, having
children, or even welcoming grandchildren. It marks the culmi-
nation of years, sometimes decades or even generations, of hard work.
It's the closing of one chapter, but it's also the opening of another.

As I reflected on this book and especially this chapter, I came to
one very clear realization: I don't sell businesses. I sell freedom for
business owners.

And freedom comes in many forms. For some, it's financial—the
money from selling the business provides the opportunity never to
have to work again. For others, it's about time—the ability to finally
stop punching the clock and start living life on your own terms.

Either way, you need a plan for what comes after the sale. That
plan starts with the immediate future. How will you handle your
post-closing transition and support period? The buyer is counting on
you for a smooth handoff. They need your insight, your experience,
and your confidence to guide them through those first critical months.
Helping them succeed ensures your legacy continues, and it helps
protect the reputation and relationships you worked so hard to build.

But your plan also needs to include *you*. You've earned a break. Maybe it's a golf trip with your buddies at a legendary resort. Perhaps it's a cruise, a family vacation, or even just a quiet week with no emails, no employees, and no pressure. Whatever it looks like, take the time. You've earned it. And don't forget to celebrate. Gather your family, your friends, and some former or retired employees. Take a moment to thank everyone who helped you along the way.

Redefining Who You Are

When you've spent decades being known as *the business owner,* that title becomes a big part of who you are. For many people, it *is* who they are. So when the business sells, there's this strange limbo period, almost like losing a piece of your identity.

I went through this myself. It took about four, maybe even five years for people—not my close friends or family, but acquaintances, people I'd run into at the country club—to stop introducing me as "the guy who owned that health insurance claims company."

It was funny, actually. To get people to update their mental Rolodex, I'd literally have to shake their hand and say, "Mark Hartmann, Mergers and Acquisitions." It became a bit of a running joke. But it highlights an important point: when you meet people, they put you in a box. "I know Tom—Tom's the widget guy. If I ever need widgets, I call Tom."

But what happens when Tom sells his company and no longer makes widgets? People have a hard time disconnecting Tom from that identity. It's human nature. So, you have to be patient with yourself and with others. It takes time for people to adjust to your new reality of no longer being *the owner.*

And you'll need to adjust, too. You're stepping into a new season of life, whether that means buying another business, consulting, teaching, mentoring, or maybe even fully retiring. The key is to approach this with the same intentionality you brought to building your business.

Don't Wait to Discover What's Next

You don't want to wait until after the sale to figure out who you are or what you're going to do next. You should be exploring that long before you close the deal. Most owners already have passions and hobbies—activities such as charity work, volunteering, or golf. But you're not going to golf five days a week, 40 hours a week, like you were working in your business. That fantasy wears off fast.

Consider what else you would like to dedicate your time and energy to. Maybe it's writing a book. Perhaps you want to teach part-time when you retire. Give it a try before you sell. Guest lecture somewhere. Volunteer to mentor a student. See how it feels. The same goes for any potential passion project—try it on for size while you still have the safety net of your business. That way, when you finally leave the closing table and step into your next chapter, you'll already have momentum.

The Power of Relationships in Retirement

Money and health matter—there's no denying that. But when it comes to whether retirement feels empty or deeply fulfilling, relationships are the deciding factor.

If you've spent most of your life getting up at 6:00 a.m., heading to work by 7:00, and staying busy until 5:00, that daily rhythm becomes ingrained. Then, one day, it stops. Suddenly, your calendar is wide open. That can be liberating, or it can feel like a void. Relationships with family, friends, and your broader community are what give those days meaning. Without them, even the biggest payday from your business sale can feel hollow.

As you plan your exit, don't just focus on the financial side. Think about how you'll stay connected. How will your role in your family evolve? What kind of friendships do you want to nurture? How do you want to contribute to your community?

If you're staying involved with your company for a transition period, that adjustment might be gradual. But if your goal is full retirement, then you need to be proactive. Build those social habits early. Join that group. Volunteer for that cause. Spend time with the people who mean the most to you.

Your Post-Sale Journey

There's no one-size-fits-all answer to finding fulfillment after the sale. I've seen just about everything through my family, friends, and clients, and it looks different for everyone. Some people dive into hobbies. Others give their time and wisdom through mentorship or consulting. Some start investing or buy another business. Others focus on philanthropy or charitable work. Whatever path you choose, ensure it aligns with your needs. Don't chase someone else's version of happiness—chase your own.

I was 42 when we sold EthiCare Advisors. I had a short transition agreement after the sale, but I already knew what I wanted to do next. I had teed myself up for my next phase of life years before the sale ever happened.

Back in 2012, five years before selling the company, I became a Certified Exit Planning Advisor (CEPA). Around the same time, I also completed the Certified Value Builder program through John

Warrillow's Value Builder System. I then earned my Certified Business Intermediary (CBI) designation through the International Business Brokers Association (IBBA) and completed the Certified Mergers & Acquisitions Professional (CM&AP) program at Kennesaw State University.

I had also tested the waters long before the sale by helping with family transactions, going back to 2008. So when I sold EthiCare, I wasn't starting from scratch—I was stepping into something I had already been building toward.

After the sale, I officially transitioned into being an M&A advisor and business broker. And to this day, I can honestly say it's been one of the most fulfilling decisions I've ever made. It gives me the freedom to choose who I work with. I get to partner with people I genuinely like—owners who are realistic about their goals, especially when it comes to valuation.

If someone tells me their business is worth $12 million and I know it's worth $6 million, we're not on the same page. And that's okay. I'd rather walk away from a deal than waste time chasing something that doesn't align with reality. That clarity—and the ability to choose— have been significant reasons why I've thrived since selling EthiCare in 2017.

Being an M&A advisor also gives me flexibility. I don't have to be in an office from nine to five, Monday through Friday. I can run my practice from anywhere in the world, thanks to technology. That ability to control my schedule and my environment is something I value tremendously. Sure, some days drive me crazy—when deals go sideways or buyers and sellers are butting heads—but I can honestly say I love what I do. And when you love what you do, it doesn't feel like work.

That's what I'd encourage you to think about. You don't have to stop working altogether—you have to redefine what "work" means to you. Perhaps you would like to stay in the industry as a consultant or mentor. Today's technology makes it easier than ever. Between Zoom, Teams, and WhatsApp, you can communicate and work from virtually anywhere there's Wi-Fi. Maybe you want to invest in new ventures or start something small and hands-on again. If you're considering a new business, think hard about what you want your life to look like day to day. If you're drawn to something like retail, understand that it requires physical presence and management. If you plan to travel three or four months a year, it's best to have strong management and systems in place. Or maybe you want to do something completely different—something you've always loved but never had the time for.

Some owners sell businesses they never truly loved. Maybe it was a family company they felt obligated to run. Selling gives them the freedom to pursue what they want, finally. Others sell businesses they built from scratch and want to return to what first inspired them—to roll up their sleeves again as a technician, not a CEO.

Retirement doesn't have to mean stopping. It can mean returning to purpose, to passion, to what makes you feel alive.

The Best Is Yet to Come

There's an old saying: *"Man makes plans, and God laughs."*

That saying applies to business, and it applies even more to selling one. Just because you get an LOI doesn't mean you'll see the closing table. Most sellers will go through multiple LOIs before they find the right deal.

But please don't lose sight of the *why*. Don't forget why you're selling your business, and what you plan to do next. This is a once-in-a-lifetime event. You only sell your business once—make it count.

Build the right team. Sell smart. Stay grounded in your goals.

And when that wire hits your account, don't think of it as the end. It's the beginning of something new. **The best is yet to come.**

KEY TAKEAWAYS

- Selling your business is the gateway to freedom, whether that means time, financial independence, or the chance to live on your own terms.
- Your identity will evolve after the sale, and that's okay. Be intentional about redefining who you are and give both yourself and others time to adjust.
- Don't wait until the deal is done to discover what's next—test-drive new passions, pursuits, or roles while you still have your business as a safety net.
- True fulfillment in retirement stems from meaningful relationships and a sense of purpose. Stay connected, engaged, and contributing to something that matters.
- The sale isn't the end of your story—it's the start of your next chapter. Plan it well, stay grounded in your "why," and remember: the best is yet to come.

EPILOGUE

"Your business is only as valuable as its ability to run without you."
— John Warrillow, *Built to Sell*

Congratulations! You now have the knowledge and a practical playbook to exit on your terms, protect your legacy, and claim the freedom you've been building toward for years. You've shifted from hope to a plan, aligning your company with what buyers value most: profitability, predictability, and transferability. This will allow it to thrive without you.

But remember this: waiting is gambling. You can't time the market, and the Five Ds—distress, divorce, disagreement, disability, and death—don't ask permission. Delay invites lower valuations, tougher terms, and preventable stress in due diligence.

So take the next step. Book a confidential readiness call to get a current valuation, a sellability assessment, and a short list of priorities tailored to your business.

Here's your simple 1-2-3 roadmap to move forward:

1. **Know your value.** Commission a valuation and answer the deal-ready questions about your finances, owner dependence, and emotional readiness.

2. **De-risk and document.** Diversify your customers, lock in contracts with assignability, multi-thread key accounts, establish SOPs and KPIs, and ensure your financials are CPA-reviewed.

3. **Build your dream deal team.** Surround yourself with an experienced M&A advisor, transaction attorney, and CPA—and set weekly deal cadences through LOI, diligence, and close.

As you execute, you'll create a business that commands better terms and gives you options after the sale—consulting, mentoring, investing, or fully retiring—so when the wire hits, it's the start of your next chapter, not the end of your story.

You only sell your business once—make it count.

Don't Just Read About Exit Mastery – Begin Yours Today

Claim your no-cost *"Exit Strategy Discovery Call"* — a private, one-on-one session where we'll:

- Diagnose your business's hidden potential (and overlooked risks)
- Reveal what buyers will really pay for (not just theoretical valuation)
- Map your fastest path to a lucrative exit — aligned with your goals, timeline, and legacy

This conversation isn't a pitch — it's a clarity session for entrepreneurs (especially those valued at $1M–$25M) who are committed to selling intelligently, protecting their team, and moving into the next chapter with confidence.

Inspire Change Beyond Your Own Business

Invite Mark Hartmann to speak to your organization, association, or peer group about how entrepreneurs can transition with clarity, confidence, and purpose.

Schedule your call here:
HartmannRhodes.com/Discovery

Let's turn your exit from theory into
real results — on your terms.

APPENDIX A

Glossary of Deal Terms

Asset Purchase Agreement (APA) —
An agreement between a business owner and a business buyer in which the buyer purchases certain business assets (and may assume certain liabilities) of the company without buying the company's stock or membership interests.

Assignability (contract assignability) —
Contract provisions allowing certain customer, vendor, and employment agreements to be transferred from the business owner to the business buyer at closing.

Change-of-control (provisions) —
Certain contract provisions that trigger rights, consents, or actions when a company's ownership changes hands.

Data room —
An online, organized directory of due diligence documents.

Death by a thousand cuts —
A business buyer tactic of raising many small issues or asks that cumulatively erode value.

Due diligence —
A comprehensive review to validate the business. Business buyers will deeply examine financial, legal, operational, tax, HR, and other areas of the company, depending on the industry.

Earn-out —
Contingent future payments to the seller that are tied to certain performance targets.

EBITDA —
It stands for Earnings Before Interest, Taxes, Depreciation, and Amortization. This is a core metric used in business valuation. It is pronounced "E-BIT-DA".

Financial buyer —
An ROI-driven business acquirer focused on cash flow and eventual exit.

Last-minute discovery —
A purported new issue raised right before closing to force concessions.

Letter of Intent (LOI) —
A (mostly) binding terms sheet agreement between the business owner and buyer outlining price, structure, key terms, timelines, and exclusivity.

No-shop (exclusivity) —
An LOI clause restricting the business owner from soliciting other offers during due diligence.

Pitch book (Confidential Information Memorandum, CIM) —
The marketing document prepared by the M&A advisor or business broker that tells the company's story and discloses known issues to reduce retrade attempts.

Post-LOI nibbles —

Serial small requests after signing an LOI that cumulatively erode value.

Private equity (PE) —

Institutional capital that acquires companies to grow and exit, oftentimes in the form of roll-ups. PE usually targets companies with >$1M in EBITDA.

Representations & warranties —

Statements and assurances made by the parties in the definitive agreement that can survive closing and carry remedies if untrue.

Retrade —

An attempt to reduce the purchase price or change terms after LOI, often during due diligence. Sometimes it's legitimate, other times it's gamesmanship.

Roll-up —

A business strategy of acquiring and combining companies in a sector to create scale and higher exit multiples.

Seller note (seller's note) —

The business owner financed portion of the price paid over time on agreed terms.

Seller's Discretionary Earnings (SDE) —

This is an owner-operated business cash flow metric used predominantly in smaller transactions. It's EBITDA plus owner's compensation and add-backs.

Stock Purchase Agreement (SPA) —
An agreement between a business owner and a business buyer in which the buyer purchases the business owner's stock and assumes the company's assets and liabilities.

Strategic buyer —
An industry operator seeking to buy businesses to obtain synergies such as cost savings, market expansion, and competitive advantage.

Transition agreement/transition plan —
The written plan for the business owner's post-closing involvement oftentimes detailing time on site, training, introductions, and handoffs.

Valuation multiple —
The market factor applied to EBITDA or SDE to estimate value. The multiple varies by business size, industry, growth, and risks.

Walk-away (walk-away point) —
The preset line past which the seller declines further concessions.

Working capital adjustment —
The true-up mechanism that compares the delivered working capital to the agreed target at closing and adjusts the price.

Working capital peg —
This is the agreed target level of net working capital to be delivered at closing. It's the benchmark for the working capital adjustment.

ABOUT MARK HARTMANN

Mark Hartmann, MBA, is a New Jersey–based mergers and acquisitions advisor and business broker who helps owners of companies with $1 million to $25 million in revenue plan and execute successful exits.

Before advising others, Mark built, scaled, and sold his own company—a 3x Inc. 5000 honoree—giving him the owner's perspective he brings to every mandate. He understands how to create value, attract qualified buyers, and negotiate outcomes that align with an owner's goals.

Mark's academic and professional background demonstrate the range of his work. He earned an MBA in Organizational Management from Eastern University and an MS in Management from the College of Saint Elizabeth. He also completed the Certified Mergers & Acquisitions Professional (CM&AP) program at Kennesaw State University.

A committed practitioner, Mark is a Certified Business Intermediary (CBI), Certified Exit Planning Advisor (CEPA), Certified Value Builder, and Financial Modeling & Valuation Analyst.

Beyond dealmaking, Mark participates in service and professional organizations, including the International Business Brokers Association and the Exit Planning Institute. His volunteer leadership roles have included work with the Park Avenue Foundation in New Jersey.

Through HartmannRhodes, Mark combines detailed preparation with compassionate guidance—helping founders navigate the challenges of selling a lower-middle-market business and confidently step into their next chapter.